STUDENT UNIT GUIDE

NEW EDITION

AQA AS Accounting Unit 2

Financial and Management Accounting

Ian Harrison

 PHILIP ALLAN

Philip Allan, an imprint of Hodder Education, an Hachette UK company, Market Place, Deddington, Oxfordshire OX15 0SE

Orders

Bookpoint Ltd, 130 Milton Park, Abingdon, Oxfordshire OX14 4SB

tel: 01235 827827

fax: 01235 400401

e-mail: education@bookpoint.co.uk

Lines are open 9.00 a.m.–5.00 p.m., Monday to Saturday, with a 24-hour message answering service. You can also order through the Philip Allan website: www.philipallan.co.uk

ISBN 978-1-4441-7143-3

First printed 2012
Impression number 5 4 3 2
Year 2015 2014

Cover photo: Fotolia

Typeset by Integra Software Services Pvt. Ltd., Pondicherry, India

Printed in Dubai

Hachette UK's policy is to use papers that are natural, renewable and recyclable products and made from wood grown in sustainable forests. The logging and manufacturing processes are expected to conform to the environmental regulations of the country of origin.

P02076

Contents

Content Guidance

Questions & Answers

Getting the most from this book

Examiner tips

Advice from the examiner on key points in the text to help you learn and recall unit content, avoid pitfalls, and polish your exam technique in order to boost your grade.

Knowledge check

Rapid-fire questions throughout the Content Guidance section to check your understanding.

Knowledge check answers

1 Turn to the back of the book for the Knowledge check answers.

Summary

Summaries

- Each core topic is rounded off by a bullet-list summary for quick-check reference of what you need to know.

Questions & Answers

Exam-style questions

Examiner comments on the questions
Tips on what you need to do to gain full marks, indicated by the icon **e**.

Sample student answers
Practise the questions, then look at the student answers that follow each question.

Questions & Answers

Question I **Types of business ownership**

Harold currently works for Gloria in her general store. Gloria wishes to retire and Harold has agreed to purchase her business as a going concern.

He is unsure whether he should

(i) trade as a sole trader, or

(ii) enter into partnership, or

(iii) make the business a private limited company

REQUIRED

Advise Harold on the type of ownership that should be adopted when he sets up in business. (10 marks)
plus 2 marks for quality of written communication

This is a popular type of question with examiners. It tests a student's knowledge of each type of business organisation. The word 'advise' requires a judgement to be made and is therefore testing the higher-order skill of evaluation. Students must always draw written answers to a clear conclusion when analysis and evaluative trigger words are used in a question.

Student A
There are many advantages in trading as a sole trader. Harold will be his own boss and so he can make all the business decisions without consulting anyone else. It means that he can keep all the profit earned in the business and he does not have to show anyone else his financial statements.

This is a good start, showing that the student appreciates the advantages of trading as a sole trader.

However, there are a number of disadvantages. These include: Will he be able to cope? At the moment he is working only in the store — has he got the necessary management skills to actually be in charge of the whole business?

This is a perceptive point that few students would comment upon.

He will have no one to discuss action plans or decisions with and to offload any business problems that he might encounter. He will have no one to cover him if he were ill or needed a day off work. Harold must stand all losses that the business might suffer and he will have unlimited liability.

There are two good points here. An explanation of the concept of unlimited liability would have indicated that the student had not merely 'lifted' the phrase from a textbook.

34

AQA AS Accounting

Examiner commentary on sample student answers
Find out how many marks each answer would be awarded in the exam and then read the examiner comments (preceded by the icon **e**) following each student answer.

AQA AS Accounting

About this book

This student guide is an ideal resource for your revision of AQA Accounting AS Unit 2: Financial and Management Accounting. The guide has two sections:

- **Content Guidance** covers the content of Unit 2.
- **Questions and Answers** provides ten questions; each question focuses on a specific area of content. Each question is based on the format of the AS examination papers and is followed by two sample answers (an A-grade and lower-grade response) together with comments by the examiner.

You should read the relevant topic area in the Content Guidance section before you attempt a question from the Questions and Answers section. Only read the specimen answers after you have attempted the question yourself.

The Content Guidance section of this guide outlines the topic areas covered in Unit 2. This unit gives you an opportunity to develop your knowledge and understanding of financial accounting. It introduces you to some of the ways in which business performance and future plans can be measured and monitored.

It allows you to develop your ability to produce financial statements of sole traders and limited companies. You should be able to make more complex adjustments to financial statements and you should be able to show an understanding of the concepts that need to be applied when preparing financial statements and to explain how these concepts are applied in a variety of situations.

You are expected to understand how the structure of a limited company differs from that of a sole trader or a partnership. You should be able to explain why these forms of ownership are appropriate in certain circumstances and how ownership and control are exercised in each form.

You should be able to evaluate the financial strengths and weaknesses of businesses and report on their performance. You must be able to support comments with evidence based on analysing ratios calculated from the relevant financial statements. You should be able to recommend courses of action that will benefit the business and explain the consequences if action is not taken.

Aims of the AS qualification

The AS accounting course aims to encourage students to develop:

- an understanding of the importance of effective accounting information systems and an awareness of their limitations
- an understanding of the purposes, principles, concepts and techniques of accounting
- the transferable skills of numeracy, communication, ICT, application, presentation, interpretation, analysis and evaluation in an accounting context
- an appreciation of the effects of economic, legal, ethical, social, environmental and technological influences on accounting decisions
- a capacity for methodical and critical thought which serves as an end in itself as well as a basis for further study of accounting and other subjects

Content Guidance

Types of business organisation

Although you are not required to prepare the financial statements for a partnership, you are expected to know what are the advantages and the disadvantages of the form as a type of ownership.

This section of the specification is an ideal vehicle to test your evaluative skills. Do read the questions carefully and focus your answer on the precise question set by the examiner. It is useful to underline or highlight the key phrases in the question so that you do remain focused.

If a question asks you to advise a friend whether or not he or she should form a partnership or a private limited company rather than trading as a sole trader, your answer should be focused on personal advice not on the benefits to the business. Advice or a discussion should contain some form of judgement backed up by your analysis.

Sole traders

Sole traders are the most common form of business organisation. One person is responsible for conducting the business. He or she is also legally responsible for the stewardship of the business.

A sole trader benefits from certain advantages:
- The owner keeps all the profits earned by the business.
- The owner makes all the business decisions, so success or failure depends on the trader only.
- There are no complex legal procedures in setting up and running the business.
- The financial results of the business do not need to be divulged to the general public.

However, there are also a number of disadvantages in trading as a sole trader:
- The owner has to stand all business losses.
- The owner bears all the responsibilities inherent in running the business.
- The owner is liable for all the debts incurred by the business, even if this entails selling some private assets to pay them (unlimited liability).
- The business is restricted in the acquisition of further capital for expansion of the business.
- The business may involve long hours of work, and illness may affect the running of the business.
- There may be no one with whom to share problems or ideas.

Examiner tip
A common error is to use the term 'company' when describing the businesses of sole traders and partnerships. Try using the term 'business' instead. When you get used to this term you will not make this mistake again.

Knowledge check 1
A sole trader is a person who owns a business and is the only person working in that business. True or false?

Partnerships

Forming a partnership overcomes some of the disadvantages of being in business as a sole trader. The advantages of being in partnership are:

- There is access to more capital.
- Partners can share the workload.
- Partners can share problems and can pool ideas that might benefit the business.

The disadvantages of being in partnership are:

- There is less independence than being a sole trader.
- Decisions have to be agreed by all partners — the ideas of one or more partners may be frustrated by other partners.
- Partners are jointly and severally liable for all the debts incurred by the business, even if this entails selling private assets to settle the debts (unlimited liability).

Limited companies

Limited liability companies came into existence because of the need for businesses to raise capital and at the same time to give investors a degree of security.

The advantages of forming a limited company are:

- There is limited liability status for shareholders.
- The directors are able to raise larger amounts of capital for use within the company.

The disadvantages of forming a limited company are:

- Annual financial statements must be audited by professionally qualified personnel.
- Annual returns must be completed by the directors and filed with the Registrar of Companies.
- The annual filed financial statements may be inspected by the general public at Companies House.
- Companies are subject to more 'red tape' than sole traders or partnerships.
- Copies of the company's annual audited financial statements must be sent to each shareholder and debenture holder.

The act of forming a registered limited company is known as incorporation.

Ownership and control of a business

In the case of sole traders and partnerships, ownership and control rests with the same people. However, in the case of limited companies, ownership is separate from the control of the business. Ownership rests with the shareholders, whereas control of the business is in the hands of the directors of the company. The directors guide the daily business and are generally also responsible for strategic planning.

Examiner tip
Types of business organisation is a topic area often used in testing a student's evaluative skills.

Knowledge check 2
Explain the term 'jointly and severally liable'.

Shareholders in a limited company are sometimes also known as members.

Examiner tip
You should be aware and be able to discuss the advantages and disadvantages of being in business as a sole trader; you should also be able to compare and evaluate being a sole trader with being in partnership or forming a limited company.

Knowledge check 3
Explain the term 'limited liability'.

Summary

- Sole trader is the type of business that has only one owner, who controls the business.
- Sole traders form the most common type of business ownership.
- Some of the disadvantages of sole ownership and control are overcome by partnerships. However, you should also be aware that partnership adds further disadvantages.
- Both forms have unlimited liability. In the case of partnerships, there is the added dimension of all partners being responsible for all the debts of the business, no matter which partner is responsible for the debt.
- Formation of a limited company overcomes the problem posed by unlimited liability; but limited companies are subject to many more statutory regulations.
- Sole traders and businesses are controlled by the owners. Shareholders in a limited company elect directors to guide and control the business.

Accounting concepts

Accounting concepts are the basic rules that all accountants use when preparing the financial statements of a business. This ensures consistency of approach wherever and by whomever the statements are prepared. This area is popular with examiners. Questions generally outline a scenario and students are asked to explain the concept used or the concept that ought to have been used.

The concepts that could be examined include the following.

Cost

All assets and expenses are recorded in the books of account at cost since this is objective.

Example: My vintage car cost £18000. I think that it is now worth £20000. Cost of £18000 is objective but my valuation of £20000 is subjective and so should not be used.

Going concern

Unless there is information to the contrary, the accounts of the business are prepared under the assumption that the business will continue to trade in its present form for the foreseeable future. This means that all assets are valued at cost, not at what they could be sold for. If the business is going to continue to trade, the assets will not be sold and so a sale value is irrelevant.

Example: My business premises cost £200000. Similar premises have been sold last week for £240000. The amount shown on the statement of financial position will be:

	£
Premises at cost	200000

Accruals

The value of resources used by a business and the benefits derived from the use of those resources are recorded in the books of account in the financial year. The value,

Knowledge check 4

A business owns a workshop on an industrial estate. It cost £35000 several years ago. Recently an adjacent workshop was sold for £60000. How should the workshop be shown on a statement of financial position? Which concept should be applied?

Knowledge check 5

Give another name for the accruals concept.

to the business, of resources used may be different from the amounts paid during the financial year to acquire the resources.

Example: Rent paid during the financial year ended 31 March 2012 was £7200. At the year end, £800 remained unpaid for the financial year. £8000 would be shown on the income statement (the total rent for the year ended 31 March 2012) and £800 would be shown as a current liability — accrued rent (the amount outstanding at the end of the financial year).

Consistency

Consistency requires that once a method of treating information has been established, the same method should continue to be used in subsequent years. If different methods are used in different years, inter-year comparisons cannot be made reliably and any trends cannot be observed.

Example: Arthur wishes to change the annual rate of depreciation charged on his vehicles from the usual 20% (£30000) to 10% this year (£15000) to improve his reported profits. Such an action would violate the concept of consistency and make it difficult to compare this year's results with those in previous years.

Prudence

Revenues and profits are only included in the accounts when they are realised. Provision is made for all known expenses or losses when they become known.

Examples: Tariq will sign a contract for £150000 of work on 7 January next year — one week after his financial year end. He intends to include £150000 in this year's income statement. The concept of prudence does not allow this as the £150000 can be included only when the sale actually takes place.

Martin will provide £1700 to cover potential doubtful debts after scrutinising the debts outstanding at the year end.

Materiality

If the inclusion or exclusion of financial information would mislead the users of the financial statements, then the information is 'material'. The concept recognises that some types of expenditure are less important than others, so absolute precision of recording such items is not essential.

Example: A pencil eraser costs 84 pence and is expected to be used in the office for 4 years. So, technically, the eraser is a non-current asset. It should, strictly speaking, be shown on the statement of financial position as a non-current asset. In reality, it would be entered in the office expenses or sundry expenses account. This classification is unlikely to cause the financial statements to confuse the users.

The realisation concept

This states that profits are usually recognised when the title to the goods passes to a customer, not necessarily when the money (price) changes hands. A sale takes place when the goods are replaced with cash or with an asset (debtor). The realisation concept is a subset of the accruals concept.

Knowledge check 6

The agreed rent for the year is £10000. However, only £8000 has been paid in the current year. What amounts should be shown in the financial statements? Which concept should be applied?

Examiner tip

You probably already use and apply many accounting concepts in the work you are doing. Learn what the nine concepts outlined mean and how they should be applied to the problems you might encounter in your examination.

Examiner tip

When you have learned a concept, try to remember an example of its application. Sometimes an example can clarify a subject that is difficult to explain in abstract terms.

Knowledge check 7

Explain why accountants use accounting concepts when they are preparing financial statements.

Title is the legal term for ownership. If someone has the title deeds to a pocket of land, the document shows that the holder is the legal owner.

Knowledge check 8

Theo is a sole trader. He sometimes uses his business vehicle for private use. He includes the cost of fuel as a business expense as it amounts to only about £120 per month. He says that this is acceptable because he is a sole trader and it represents only a small proportion of the total amount paid annually for motor expenses. Comment on Theo's actions regarding fuel costs.

Examiner tip

Always give your answer a heading. The heading should be accurate and contain the name of the organisation. Do not use abbreviations in your heading.

The business entity concept

This says that only transactions affecting the business are recorded in the business books of account and, consequently, the financial statements. Capital introduced or withdrawn is recorded in the proprietor's capital account and drawings account.

Example: Money spent on a holiday for the proprietor cannot be included as 'office expenses' or 'travelling expenses' — this should be recorded as 'drawings'.

Objectivity

Accountants must be objective; that is, view the business and its transactions in a dispassionate way. The records should not be subject to personal bias. To avoid this, financial information should always be able to be verified by referring to a source document.

Example: Mary has inherited a Victorian ring from her Aunt Henrietta. She recently had the ring valued at a local antique shop. The proprietor valued it as being worth £200. He wished to purchase the ring for this amount but Mary said that it was Aunt Henrietta's favourite ring and that even if the antique dealer had offered her £5000 she would not have parted with it. Mary has placed a subjective value of at least £5000 on the ring. For an accountant, the objective value would be £200.

Summary

- Accounting concepts are the basic rules that are applied when financial statements are prepared.
- They should be applied when recording all financial transactions.
- This means that, wherever the statements are prepared, we know that the same basic rules have been applied.

Further adjustment to the income statements and statements of financial position of sole traders

You should be able to prepare an income statement with adjustments for accrued expenses and prepaid expenses quickly and very accurately. This is a task you should practise regularly.

Remember that all entries in the trial balance have already been recorded in the double-entry system, but all the items of 'additional information' given in a question have not been entered in the system. This means that each piece of additional information needs to be entered twice when you prepare the financial statements in answer to a question.

It is a useful exercise to show the adjustments as pluses and minuses on the question paper. However, do also show your adjustments as workings in any space provided. Do this neatly, as many students cannot read their own workings, and so make transposition errors.

Useful terms

A supplier who supplies goods for resale on credit and who is still owed money for goods is a **trade creditor**. Collectively, a number of trade creditors are known as **trade payables**. The total amount of trade payables will be shown as a current liability on a statement of financial position. Money owed for other goods and services is known as **other payables**.

A credit customer who still owes money for the goods received is a **trade debtor**. Collectively, a number of trade debtors are known as **trade receivables**. The total amount of trade receivables will be shown as a current asset on a statement of financial position. Money owed other than for goods sold is known as **other receivables**.

Example:

Extract from trial balance at 31 March 2012

	£	£
Rent and rates	4 200	
Motor expenses	8 460	
Trade receivables	23 486	
Trade payables		16 432

Additional information at 31 March 2012
(1) Rates paid in advance amounted to £340.
(2) Motor expenses due and unpaid amounted to £120.

Extract from trial balance at 31 March 2012

	£	£
Rent and rates	4 200 *(–340)*	
Motor expenses	8 460 *(+120)*	
Trade receivables	23 486 *(+340)*	
Trade payables		16 432 *(+120)*

This technique should make sure that you do not omit any of the adjustments.

The 'new' adjustments to be included in the financial statements will be of the following kinds.

Bad debts recovered

You must be able to make adjustments in the financial statements for bad debts recovered. This is fairly straightforward.

The bank account balance shown as a current asset will increase by the amount of cash recovered (or if the business is running a bank overdraft, this will reduce and be shown as a current liability) and the revenue received will be shown as an increase to the gross profit.

Example:

Baldeep's **draft** gross profit for the year ended 31 December 2012 is £73467. At that date, her bank overdraft was £912.

Four years ago, Jacques owed Baldeep £1409. Baldeep wrote Jacques' debt off as bad. Jacques has recently set up in business again and is now able to pay Baldeep the money owed.

Prepare the relevant entries in Baldeep's financial statements.

Answer:

Baldeep. Extract from the income statement for the year ended 31 December 2012

	£
Gross profit	73467
Add bad debt recovered	1409
	74876

Extract from the statement of financial position at 31 December 2012

	£
Current assets	
Bank balance	497 [(£912) + £1409]

Income due at the year end and incomes received in advance at the year end

Although this should be well within your capabilities, many students make errors. This is due, in the main, to complacency, carelessness or rushing to prepare the answer.

Talk yourself through the scenario as you prepare your workings. Remember the accruals concept. You need to account for all incomes whether received or receivable. Incomes due at the financial year end must be included in the financial statements for that year and must be shown on the statement of financial position as a receivable. Incomes paid in advance must be included in next year's income statement and must be shown in the statement of financial position as a payable.

Example:

Henry has a financial year end on 31 March 2012. He sublets part of his premises to Barack for £6000 per annum. At 31 March 2012 Barack has paid £6600 rent for the year ended 31 March 2012.

(Note: Henry's gross profit for the year ended 31 March 2012 was £99788.)

A draft is a first copy that will probably need to be amended or updated before the final version is produced.

Examiner tip
Showing both bad debts written off and bad debts recovered separately is a 'safer' method than netting out the two amounts, since you have one fewer calculation to do and are therefore eliminating one area where, in the 'heat' of the examination hall, you might make an error.

Prepare an income statement extract for the year ended 31 March 2012 and a statement of financial position extract at that date.

Answer:

Henry. Income statement extract for the year ended 31 March 2012

	£
Gross profit	99 788
Add rent receivable	6 000
	105 788

Statement of financial position extract at 31 March 2012

	£
Current liabilities	
Rent receivable paid in advance	600

Provision for doubtful debts

As you have seen in Unit 1, debtors (receivables) who will definitely not pay their debts are transferred to a bad debts account. At the end of the financial year, this account is closed with a credit entry, the 'other' entry being shown on the income statement as an expense.

As well as possibly having bad debts, there is always a risk in business that other debtors may not pay; they are doubtful debtors. At the end of a financial year, the owner/manager of a business will estimate the total amount owed by credit customers who might be unable to pay their debts.

The concept of prudence states that we should not anticipate possible profits but that we should make **provision** for likely losses. It therefore seems sensible that we should make provision in cases where there is a strong possibility that certain debtors may not settle their debts.

The provision may be based on:
- a list of debtors who it is suspected may not settle their debts
- a percentage of total receivables outstanding at the year end, based on past experience
- an age profile of outstanding debtors

Remember that the amount shown in the credit column of a trial balance for provision for doubtful debts is the amount that has accumulated over several years. Remember also that provisions are not cash; they are amounts set aside out of profits (cash and profits are not the same).

So a provision for doubtful debts is created to take account of credit customers who may not pay their debts. Any increase in the provision calculated on total receivables at the financial year end is entered in the income statement as an expense and it is added to the balance on the provision account shown in the trial balance (any reduction is entered in the income statement as an extra 'income' and is deducted from the balance on the provision account shown in the trial balance).

Knowledge check 10

Draft financial statements at the end of year 1: gross profit £123 450; profit for the year £75 800; trade receivables £10 500; balance on provision for doubtful debts account £400. Provision for doubtful debts is 4% per annum.

Calculate the amount for provision for doubtful debts to be shown in an income statement for the year ended year 1.

A **provision** is an amount set aside out of profits for a known expense, the amount of which is uncertain.

Knowledge check 11

In which ledger would you expect to find (a) a provision for doubtful debts account; (b) a bad debts account? Which concept is being applied when a provision is made for doubtful debts?

Example:

Extract from Jack's trial balance at 29 February 2012

	£	£
Trade receivables	19 500	
Provision for doubtful debts		400

Jack wishes to make provision for doubtful debts based on 3% of receivables outstanding at 29 February 2012.

(a) Calculate the amount to be shown as an expense for provision for doubtful debts in an income statement for the year ended 29 February 2012.

(b) Prepare a statement of financial position extract at 29 February 2012 showing entries for trade receivables and provision for doubtful debts.

Answer:

(a) The entry as an expense would be:

	£
Provision for doubtful debts	185

(b)   **Statement of financial position extract at 28 February 2012**

	£	£
Current assets		
Trade receivables	19 500	
Provision for doubtful debts	585	18 915

Depreciation

Non-current assets are purchased by a business in order to generate profits. They will be used by a business for more than one financial year and so will yield profits for the business over several years.

Some resources used by a business are used up in one accounting period; they are revenue expenses (goods purchased for resale, diesel for delivery vehicles, staff skills etc.). Other resources (premises, machinery and delivery vehicles) will be used up over a number of accounting periods; they are capital expenditure.

Since the benefits from capital expenditure will be derived over a number of years, it seems sensible to charge part of those expenditures over the years — the accruals concept again.

The total cost of a non-current asset is never charged to an income statement in the year of purchase. The cost is spread over the years of use in order to reflect, in each of the years, the cost of the asset used in that year.

Depreciation is the apportioning of the cost of a non-current asset over its useful lifetime.

Depreciation measures the wearing out of a non-current asset caused by:

- use
- the passage of time
- obsolescence

Remember that the annual depreciation charge to an income statement is only an estimate. The 'true' depreciation figure will be known only when the asset ceases to be used and is disposed of. However, it is prudent to make a charge against profits for each accounting period.

The estimate for the annual charge requires four factors to be taken into account:
- the cost of the asset
- the estimated useful economic life of the asset
- the estimated residual value of the asset
- the method of calculation

You have already used the straight-line method. This requires the same amount to be charged to an income statement over the lifetime of the non-current asset.

The formula is: $\dfrac{\text{cost of non-current asset – any residual value}}{\text{estimated number of years' use}}$

Using the reducing balance method, the estimate for the annual charge does not take into account the residual value at the end of the asset's life. A fixed percentage is applied to the cost of the asset in the first year of ownership. The same percentage is applied in subsequent years to the **carrying amount** of the asset.

You must be able to prepare a provision for depreciation account. The account will appear to be similar whichever method is used; only the amount to be transferred to the income statement as an expense will be different.

Example:

A machine is purchased for £18000 at the start of **year 0**. The machine is expected to have a useful economic life of 5 years and will then have an estimated scrap value of £1000.

Prepare a provision for depreciation account using:
(a) the straight-line method
(b) the reducing balance method at 40% per annum

Answer:

(a) Provision for depreciation of machinery account

	£		£
		Yr 0 Inc stat	3400
Yr 1 Bal c/d	6800	Yr 1 Inc stat	3400
	6800		6800
		Yr 2 Bal b/d	6800
Yr 2 Bal c/d	10200	Yr 2 Inc stat	3400
	10200		10200
		Yr 3 Bal b/d	10200
		Yr 3 Inc stat	3400

(b) Provision for depreciation of machinery account

	£		£
		Yr 0 Inc stat	7200
Yr 1 Bal c/d	11520	Yr 1 Inc stat	4320
	11520		11520
		Yr 2 Bal b/d	11520
Yr 2 Bal c/d	14112	Yr 2 Inc stat	2592
	14112		14112
		Yr 3 Bal b/d	14112
		Yr 3 Inc stat	1555

Calculations for the reducing balance annual charge:

Year 0 18000 × 40% = 7200   Year 1 18000 − 7200 = 10800 (× 40%)

Year 2 18000 − 11520 = 6480 × (40%)   Year 3 18000 − 14112 = 3888 (× 40%)

Examiner tip

All non-current assets with a finite life should be depreciated. So the only non-current asset that should not be depreciated is land, since land has an infinite life.

The **carrying amount** is the cost of a non-current asset as it appears in the general ledger, less the total depreciation charged on the asset to date.

Year 0 is the term used for the present time.

Knowledge check 12

The reducing balance method of providing for depreciation always gives a more accurate value for the carrying amount of a non-current asset than using the straight-line method. True or false?

Knowledge check 13

The carrying amount shown on a statement of financial position shows how much the asset should be sold for at that date. True or false?

Aggregate depreciation is the total depreciation to date.

As you can see, the ledger accounts are prepared in the same way, only the annual charges are different.

The words 'expected' or 'estimated' are frequently used when discussing depreciation. When a non-current asset is sold it is unlikely that the sum received will exactly match the carrying amount. This means that, when a non-current asset is sold, it is likely that a profit or loss on the carrying amount will be shown.

You will need to know how to prepare a non-current asset disposal account.

Example:

Iain Benn provides the following information from his general ledger:

Machinery account	Provision for depreciation of machinery account
31 March 12 Bal b/d 120000	31 March 12 Bal b/d 70000

Note: Remember, do not use abbreviations in your answers.

Earlier in the year, Iain sold a machine for £4000. He has entered the cash received in the cash book but has made no other entries in his ledgers.

The machine cost £25000 some years ago. The **aggregate depreciation** relating to the machine amounted to £20000.

Prepare a machinery disposal account recording the sale of the machine.

Answer:

Machinery disposal account

Machinery	25000	Provision for depreciation of machinery	20000
		Cash	4000
	25000	Income statement (loss)	1000
	25000		25000

The process is:
- Debit disposal account with the cost of the asset   Credit asset account
- Debit provision for depreciation account with the
  total depreciation relating to the asset sold   Credit disposal account
- Debit cash received from the sale   Credit disposal account
- *Debit disposal account with profit on disposal *OR*   *Credit disposal account
  with loss on disposal

*Either of these items is a balancing item. This entry will appear in the income statement. A loss will be included as an 'expense'. A profit will be added to gross profit.

Classifying expenditure and incomes into capital and revenue categories

- Capital expenditure is spending on non-current assets or their improvement.
- Revenue expenditure is spending on the everyday running costs of a business.

- Capital income is derived from sources other than the core activity of the business.
- Revenue income is derived from the everyday activities of the business.

Capital expenditure and income will not be entered in an income statement and so will not affect the reported profits of the business. Revenue expenditure and income are entered in an income statement and therefore do have an effect on the reported profits. Misclassification of either capital or revenue items will corrupt profits and make the information shown in a statement of financial position incorrect.

> The core activity is the main activity of the business. For example, the core activity of your local supermarket is the provision of general retailing. The selling of national lottery tickets by the store is not its core activity.

Summary

- Any additional information given in a question requires two entries in your answer.
- In an income statement, debtors who will definitely not pay are written off as bad debts.
- A provision for doubtful debts is created to take into account credit customers who may not pay their debts.
- In an income statement, any increase in the provision is included as an expense. Any decrease in the provision is included as an 'income'.
- Bad debts recovered are included in an income statement as an income.
- Incomes due at the end of a financial year are termed as 'other receivables' and shown in a statement of financial position as a current asset. Any incomes paid in advance are termed 'other payables' and shown as a current liability.
- Depreciation is provided on all non-current assets with the exception of land.
- A provision for depreciation represents the use of a non-current asset during its ownership. It is an application of the accruals concept.
- The two main methods used to calculate a provision for depreciation are the straight-line method and the reducing balance method.
- Whichever method is used by a business, the provision for depreciation account will look similar, only the annual charge will be different.
- Aggregate depreciation is the total depreciation to date. If this amount is deducted from the cost of the non-current asset, the result is the carrying amount.
- When an asset is scrapped or sold, a profit or loss on disposal generally occurs. Questions may require an account or a calculation as the answer. Always give examiners what they request.
- Revenue expenditure is spending on everyday running costs of a business. Revenue incomes are generated by the usual activities of a business.
- Capital expenditure is spending on non-current assets or their improvement. Capital income is derived from sources other than the usual activities.

Internal financial statements of limited companies

You should be able to explain several terms in common use when referring to limited companies.

Limited liability means that the liability of shareholders for the debts of a limited company of which they are members is restricted to the amount they agreed to subscribe. For example, if a person agrees to purchase 100 £1 ordinary shares for £1.50 each, once they have paid £1500 they are not liable to make any further payments should the company go into liquidation.

> **Knowledge check 16**
>
> Which of the following financial transactions are examples of capital expenditure for a business: (a) payment of insurance premiums; (b) purchase of car for own private use; (c) purchase of new office equipment; (d) purchase of second-hand office equipment?

Authorised share capital sets the upper limit to the number of shares the company may issue. The figure can only be exceeded with the approval of existing shareholders. The authorised share capital must be shown in the published financial statements of the company. The details of the number, classes and nominal values must be shown.

Issued share capital states the nominal share capital which has been issued to the shareholders. The issued share capital cannot exceed the authorised share capital.

Equity is the term used to describe the permanent issued share capital of a company. It comprises ordinary shares and irredeemable preferred shares.

Ordinary shares represent the ownership of a company. They are often referred to as 'equity capital' since each share earns an equal share of any profits earned by the company. Every limited company has ordinary shares and so they are the most common type of share issued by limited companies.

Preferred shares usually carry a fixed rate of dividend and are entitled to repayment in the event of the company being wound up. They have preferential rights to dividends but only if profits are high enough.

Capital reserves are amounts set aside out of profits that are not provisions. However, they are not created out of operating profits and are therefore not available for transfer back into retained earnings — so, they are not available for cash dividend purposes. They may be distributed to shareholders in the form of bonus shares.

Revenue reserves are profits that have been retained in the business to strengthen the financial position of the company. They are a very important source of finance for limited companies. Revenue reserves are available for both cash dividends and the issue of bonus shares.

Shareholders' funds are made up of the share capital of the company plus all reserves.

Remember that reserves are profits set aside; they are not cash.

Limited companies also raise finance by borrowing.

Debentures are long-term loans received by the company. A legal document records the loan. The company pays a fixed rate of interest to the holder of the bond. Debentures are usually for a fixed time period. '7% Debentures 2024' pay the lender(s) 7% interest each year and are redeemable in 2024. Debentures are usually secured by a fixed charge on a particular asset or by a floating charge on all the assets of the company. If the company was wound up or failed to pay the interest due, the holders could sell the asset(s) and recoup the amount outstanding.

Term loans from a bank or some other financial institution carry a fixed rate of interest and, as with debentures, interest must be paid whether or not the company is profitable.

Mortgages are capital obtained by mortgaging assets. The title to the assets is held by the mortgagor. Repayments (capital and interest) are spread over the life of the mortgage.

You must be able to evaluate the various ways that a limited company may choose to raise finance. You may be asked to advise the directors of a limited company on the most appropriate ways to raise capital to expand or secure the position of the company. You may be asked to advise a potential investor on which type of security to purchase as an investment. Remember to focus your answer on the question set by the examiner.

Revaluation

Many limited companies revalue their land and buildings upwards in order to reflect an increase in the value of these assets and to ensure that the statement of financial position shows the permanent change in the capital structure of the company.

If the value of the company's assets are increased then there must be a corresponding increase in the company's reserves (the accounting equation must always balance). The revaluation reserve is a capital reserve and is therefore not available for cash dividend purposes. This creation of a revaluation reserve should clearly illustrate to you that reserves are not cash.

Remember that revalued assets must be depreciated on the revalued amount that is their new carrying amount. This is why the only meaningful definition of depreciation is the one given on page 14. The process is to show a carrying amount that reflects the revalued value. This will mean increasing the amount shown in the asset account and writing off the depreciation to date.

Example:

Statement of financial position extract 31 January 2012

	£	£
Non-current assets		
Land and buildings at cost	170000	
Depreciation to date	80000	90000

The land and buildings are revalued on 1 February 2012 at £200000.

Prepare the appropriate accounts to record the revaluation of land and buildings.

Answer:

Land and buildings account					
Balance b/d	170000				
Revaluation reserve	30000				

Depreciation of land and buildings account			
Revaluation reserve	80000	Balance b/d	80000

Revaluation reserve	
Depreciation of land and buildings account	80000
Land and buildings account	30000

Reserves are amounts set aside out of profits that are not provisions.

The accounting equation recognises that the total assets owned by a business are always equal to the claims against the business.

It can be stated as Non-current assets + current assets = owners' capital + non-current liabilities + current liabilities.

A revaluation reserve is created when the directors of a limited company increase the value of non-current assets. It is a capital reserve and as such cannot be used for distribution as cash dividends.

Capital reserves are not derived from operating profits and so are not available for cash dividend purposes.

Examiner tip

It is a common error made by examination candidates to say that reserves are money set asde for future use: they are not. Never state that reserves are cash. They are past profits 'ploughed back' into a company.

Examiner tip
Learn the differences between a rights issue and a bonus issue of shares. The topic is popular with examiners.

Rights issue

A rights issue of shares is offered to existing shareholders. The right is to purchase a number of shares based on the individual shareholder's present holding. The rights issue might be one new share for every five shares already held; one new share for every twelve shares already held, etc.

The right to purchase the new shares can be sold or given to another person if the shareholder does not wish to exercise the right. The issue price is usually a little lower than the current market price since the company does not have the same administrative expenses to pay.

The effect that a rights issue has on the company statement of financial position is exactly the same as the effect that any other share issue has. Companies use rights issues to raise further capital, for example in 2008 HBOS used a rights issue to raise more capital.

Example:

The following is the summarised statement of financial position of Smithers Ltd at 30 April 2012:

	£	£
Non-current assets		160000
Current assets excluding bank	18500	
Bank	1500	
	20000	
Current liabilities	15000	5000
		165000
Equity		
Ordinary shares of 50p each		75000
Retained earnings		90000
		165000

On 30 April Smithers Ltd made a rights issue of one new ordinary share for every three held at a price of £1.50 each.

The issue was completed on 30 April 2012.

Prepare a statement of financial position at 30 April 2012 immediately after completion of the rights issue.

Answer:

Smithers Ltd summarised statement of financial position at 30 April 2012

	£	£	
Non-current assets		160000	
Current assets excluding bank	18500		
Bank	76500		(1500 + 75000)
	95000		
Current liabilities	15000	80000	
		240000	

	£	£
Equity		
Ordinary shares of 50p each		100000 *(75000 + 25000)*
Share premium		50000
Retained earnings		90000
		240000

Bonus issue

A bonus issue of shares is issued to existing shareholders in proportion to the individual shareholder's present holding. The reserves of the company are used to fund the issue.

Company reserves provide permanent finance for a company, so the transfer to share capital is a book entry and has no effect on the capital structure of the company. Total equity remains unchanged and no cash has changed hands.

Example:

The summarised statement of financial position of Burns Ltd at 30 April 2012 is given as follows.

	£	£
Non-current assets		200000
Current assets excluding bank	40000	
Current liabilities	20000	20000
		220000
Equity		
Ordinary shares of £1 each		100000
Share premium		70000
Retained earnings		50000
		220000

On 30 April 2012 the company issued one business share for every two ordinary shares held. It is company policy to maintain reserves in their most flexible form.

Prepare a statement of financial position at 30 April 2012 immediately after the bonus issue of shares.

Answer:

Burns Ltd summarised statement of financial position at 30 April 2012

	£	£
Non-current assets		200000
Current assets excluding bank	40000	
Current liabilities	20000	20000
		220000

Examiner tip

A statement that 'it is company policy to maintain reserves in their most flexible form' means that you should use capital reserves before revenue reserves when issuing bonus shares. Capital reserves have limited uses.

	£	£
Equity		
Ordinary shares of £1 each		150000
Share premium		20000
Retained earnings		50000
		220000

Note that the share premium account has been used to fund the issue since the capital reserve is restricted in its use. The retained earnings do not carry the same restrictions: they are much more flexible as a reserve.

Examination questions often ask you to complete both share issue processes almost simultaneously — an unlikely event in the real world but a device that examiners may use to make sure that you understand how to deal with each type of share issue. Do not try to do both types of issue in one attempt; treat the question in two parts. Complete one type of issue before you start on the next type.

Questions will require you only to adjust a given statement of financial position or an extract from a statement of financial position. Show all your adjustments as workings so that, if you make any errors, you could score part marks for any correct adjustments made.

Preparation of the internal income statements and statements of financial position of limited companies

You should be able to prepare the income statement, including an appropriation section for a limited company, and make provision for any tax liability. You should also be able to prepare a statement of changes in equity.

Provision for corporation tax is deducted from the current year's profit and, because the tax will be paid in the following financial year, it will appear in the statement of financial position, at the end of the year, as a current liability.

Example:

The directors of Jasdeep Gahir Ltd supply the following information after the first year of trading.

Trial balance at 31 December 2012

	Dr	Cr
	£	£
Operating profit for the year		230000
Non-current assets	300000	
Current assets	100000	
Dividends paid	27000	
Ordinary shares of £1 each		150000
6% debentures		50000
Debenture interest paid	3000	
	430000	430000

AQA AS Accounting

Examiner tip

A bonus issue has no effect on the equity of a limited company. The process transfers funds from reserves to share capital. Check this by using the accounting equation:

Non-current assets + current assets = owners' capital + non-current liabilities + current liabilities

Knowledge check 17

Explain the difference between a rights issue and a bonus issue of shares.

A **statement of changes in equity** shows all changes to the components comprising equity during the year. The components include permanent share capital and all the reserves.

The directors wish to provide for corporation tax due £72 000.

Prepare an income statement for the year ended 31 December 2012 and a summarised statement of financial position at that date.

Answer:

Jasdeep Gahir Ltd. Income statement extract for the year ended 31 December 2012

	£
Operating profit	230 000
Interest paid	3 000
Profit before tax	227 000
Tax	72 000
Profit for the year	155 000

Statement of changes in equity

	£
Retained earnings	
Balance at 1 January 2012	—
Profit for the year	155 000
	155 000
Dividends paid	27 000
Balance at 31 December 2012	128 000

Summarised statement of financial position extract at 31 December 2012

	£
Non-current assets	300 000
Current assets	100 000
Current liabilities	
Taxation	(72 000)
	328 000
Non-current liabilities	
6% debentures	(50 000)
	278 000
Equity	
Share capital	150 000
Retained earnings	128 000
Total equity	278 000

- You should be able to explain the terms listed in the text. You should also be able to evaluate the various ways that a limited company is able to raise additional finance.
- When a limited company increases the value of non-current assets as shown in a statement of financial position, a corresponding increase in equity must be shown by creating a capital reserve — a revaluation reserve.
- A revaluation reserve is not available for distribution of cash dividends.
- Future provisions for depreciation of non-current assets will be based on the revalued figure.
- Both rights issues and bonus issues of shares are available to existing shareholders. Both are given as a percentage of the shareholders' present holding.

- Rights issues are used to raise more finance. A bonus issue is used to restore a position where share capital is 'out of step' with the asset base of the company.
- You should be able to prepare the internal financial statements of a limited company. They are essentially similar to all the other financial statements you have already prepared. However, you must include corporation tax and should prepare a statement of changes in equity. In the place of capital accounts you should include equity (permanent share capital and reserves).

Ratio analysis

Ratio analysis is a method of analysing the results of a business in order to judge its performance. Financial statements contain much information, but these raw data do not reveal how good or bad the performance has been.

It would be difficult to compare the raw data produced in two sets of financial statements from businesses of very different sizes. The raw data produced for Joe's mini-mart, with one retail outlet, cannot easily be compared with the raw data extracted from the financial statements of, say, Tesco plc.

Similarly, it would be difficult to compare the underlying trends in the raw data produced in 2001 with those of 2008 or 2012, because of changes in the value of money with time. So results are converted into percentages that can be more meaningfully compared.

Remember that ratios are always used as a comparative device. Do not say that 38% is good; always state that 38% is better or worse than the results:
- shown last year
- budgeted
- of a similar business
- of the sector as a whole

'Ratio' is a generic term that is applied to many different calculations (percentages, time, ratios etc.). The relationship between figures gives a better indication of the efficiency and effectiveness of the organisation.

The ratios calculated are needed by many users of financial statements, including owners, managers, bank managers, revenue and customs, potential investors etc. Remember that the users of the accounting information are interested in assessing whether or not the business will continue to trade into the future and how successful

it might be. This depends in the short term on the ability of the business to generate the following:
- positive cash flows — its liquidity
- positive profits — its profitability

Businesses rely on liquidity for survival in the short term. They rely on profitability for survival in the long term.

The accounting information in the form of ratios is used to compare the results of:
- a business over a number of years
- two or more similar businesses

In the examination, questions will generally be based on the two scenarios described above. In reality, some users — like the owner/managers and bank managers — may also compare actual performance with the performance predicted in budgeted figures.

You need to be able to comment on whether the results are better or worse than:
- trends shown in previous years' results
- results of the business in question compared with the results of another business in the same business sector
- the average results of a number of businesses in the sector

Questions in examinations will require you to:
- calculate some ratios
- interpret them
- generally evaluate them

The strategy to adopt in answering such questions is:
- Always state the formula you have used in full, for example:

$$\text{gross profit margin} = \frac{\text{gross profit}}{\text{sales}} \times 100$$

Do not abbreviate the words 'gross profit' or 'sales' and always include × 100.
- Do the calculation and always include the description for your answer, for example 72%; 18 days; 42 times.
- Compare your results with the comparative results, for example 2012 results show an improvement on the 2008 results, Boris's results are better than Ken's results.
- Quantify the differences in the figures being compared, for example 2012 results show an improvement on the 2008 results; the gross profit margin has increased by 25%; it was 40% in 2008, in 2012 it was 50% (an increase of 10% on the original of 40% so 10 ÷ 40 × 100 = 25%).
- If possible, give reasons for the improvement or deterioration. This may not be possible if the scenario given is limited.

Gross profit margin shows how much the business earns from each £1 of sales. So, a gross profit margin of 60% means that for every £1 of sales, 60 pence is gross profit. (Remember, you cannot say whether this result is good or bad; you need to compare it with some other result. 60% is better than 54% but 60% is poor compared with 75%.)

The formula to be used is: $\dfrac{\text{gross profit}}{\text{sales}} \times 100$

Examiner tip

It is important that you learn the formulae listed in the specification. Practise them regularly. There are only eleven of them. Write them down on a card and learn three or four each week. Do this with a friend and test each other regularly.

Gross profit mark-up tells you how much is added to the cost of sales figure to give the selling price. So, a gross profit mark-up of 150% means that £1 cost of sales will earn £2.50.

The formula to be used is: $\dfrac{\text{gross profit}}{\text{cost of sales}} \times 100$

Rate of inventory turnover tells you how quickly, on average, goods are being sold. So, an inventory turnover figure of '7 times' or '52.14 days' tells you that goods held are being sold on average every 53 days. Once again, unless you know the results of other businesses or other years, you cannot comment on how good or bad this figure is. Clearly, the greater the number of times that inventory is turned over in a year the better, because in each 'bundle' of goods held there is an element of profit and cash tied up.

The formula to be used is: $\dfrac{\text{cost of sales}}{\text{average inventory held}}$

Overheads in relation to turnover tells you how much of each £1 of sales is taken up paying the everyday running expenses of the business. So, an overhead-to-turnover ratio of 17% tells you that out of every £1 of sales, 17p goes towards paying the wages, rent, motor expenses etc. of the business.

The formula to be used is: $\dfrac{\text{total expenses}}{\text{sales}} \times 100$

It can also be calculated by gross profit margin less net profit margin.

Profit for the year in relation to turnover (profit for the year margin) tells you how much of each £1 of sales is earned by the business for expansion purposes or for the proprietor (in the case of a limited company, how much is available to pay corporation tax and dividends and to plough back into the company). So, profit for the year margin of 12% means that the business earned 12 pence out of every £1 of sales after all expenses have been paid.

The formula to be used is: $\dfrac{\text{profit for the year before interest}}{\text{sales}} \times 100$

For a limited company, the formula to be used is:

$$\dfrac{\text{profit for the year before interest and tax}}{\text{sales}} \times 100$$

Return on capital employed measures the profit for the year earned in relation to the total amount of money invested in the business by all the providers of long-term finance. The providers of long-term finance include the proprietors, the providers of term loans and debenture holders. So, a return on capital employed of 20% means that, for every £1 invested, the business earns 20p.

The formula to be used is:

$$\dfrac{\text{profit for the year before interest (and tax for a limited company)}}{\text{capital employed}} \times 100$$

Note that some accountants use capital employed at the start of the year, while some use capital employed at the end of the year. Some use an average of the capital employed at the start of the year and the end of the year. Choose only one of these three and stick to it always — provided you state the formula that you have used you will get the marks.

Net current asset ratio (current ratio) reveals how much cover the business has for every £1 owed by the business. This is one of the 'true' ratios and should always be expressed as such — for example 1.7:1. This means that for every £1 owed as current liabilities, the business can cover this with £1.70 of current assets. 4.3:1 means that for every £1 owed, the business has £4.30 in current assets. There is no ideal ratio so do not state that this ratio 'should be' 2:1. Different businesses work with very different amounts of cover. As usual, compare your own results with those given in the question for previous years or with other businesses.

The formula to be used is: $\dfrac{\text{current assets}}{\text{current liabilities}} : 1$

Liquid capital ratio (acid test ratio) shows how much cover the business has, after excluding inventory, for every £1 owed by the business. Again this is a true ratio, i.e. something:1. A liquid capital ratio of 0.76:1 means that the business has only 76p of liquid assets for every £1 owed as current liabilities. This is a comparative figure and the ideal ratio will vary from business to business.

The formula to be used is: $\dfrac{\text{current assets less inventory}}{\text{current liabilities}} : 1$

Trade receivables collection period (average collection period) measures the time, on average, that trade receivables take to settle their debts. Care must be taken with this measurement since it may conceal debts that have been outstanding for a considerable time.

The formula to be used is: $\dfrac{\text{trade receivables}}{\text{credit sales}} \times 365$

If your calculation results in a decimal point, always round up — so 37.18 days becomes 38 days.

Trade payables payment period (average payment period) measures the time taken, on average, for a business to pay its trade payables.

The formula to be used is: $\dfrac{\text{trade payables}}{\text{credit purchases}} \times 365$

Generally, the trade receivables collection period should be shorter than the trade payables payment period.

Gearing measures the relationship between fixed cost capital and total capital. It shows how reliant the business is on 'outside' finance:
- Gearing is said to be low when the ratio is less than 50%.
- It is said to be neutral when the ratio is 50%.
- Gearing is high when the ratio is in excess of 50%.

Knowledge check 18

The following information relates to a business at 31 December 2012: inventory £48 000; trade receivables £25 000; bank overdraft £6000; trade payables £12 000.

Calculate (a) the net current asset ratio (b) the liquid capital ratio.

Knowledge check 19

The following information relates to a business for the year ended 30 November 2012: sales £250000, of which 20% are cash sales; trade payables £12000; trade receivables £15000.

Calculate the average collection period for the year ended 30 November 2012.

Examiner tip

Give your answers to two decimal places or to the number of decimal places given in the data to be used for comparative purposes.

Knowledge check 20

The following information relates to a company at 31 May 2012: issued ordinary shares £350000; 7% preferred shares £100000; 5% debentures (2028) £50000; capital reserves £70000; revenue reserves £280000.

Calculate the gearing ratio at 31 May 2012. State whether the company is a high-geared or low-geared business.

The formula to be used is:

$$\frac{\text{fixed cost capital}}{\text{total capital employed}} \times 100 = \frac{\text{long-term loans + preferred share capital}}{\text{long-term loans + preferred share capital} + \text{ordinary share capital + all reserves}} \times 100$$

You must be able to extract the relevant information from a set of financial statements given in a question, or from a set of financial statements that you have prepared as part of an answer. Questions could feature the data relevant to the statements of sole traders and/or limited companies.

You will be required to state the formula that you have used, calculate your answer, and compare the ratios with those of another time period or with those of another business or set of businesses. Remember that your comments must say 'better' or 'worse', 'improved' or 'deteriorated' or some similar comment. 'Higher' or 'lower' is not good enough.

Examiner tip

Always give the formula that you are using. Always state the 'units' that are being used. For example %; days; times.

You will have to reach a conclusion and make a reasoned judgement. Ratio questions are always evaluative. Questions set will either require a judgement as to which business is more successful (and where possible why), or advice for a potential investor as to which business is the better to invest in.

You must be aware that there are limitations in the use of financial statements and any ratios calculated from those statements. The limitations are:
- the use of historic cost in preparing data
- the use of past results
- published limited company accounts do not show the full picture
- only monetary aspects of the business are shown
- it is extremely difficult to compare like with like
- externalities are constantly changing
- different businesses have different structures, accounting policies etc.

Knowledge check 21

Identify two weaknesses in using ratios to evaluate the performance of a business.

Despite these limitations and problems of comparability, the data gained from the financial statements and ratio analysis are the best bases available for assessing comparative performance.

Cash versus profits

You must be aware of the difference between cash and profits.

Cash is money. It is a measure of the financial activities of a business in terms of cash receipts and payments without recognising accruals, prepayments, inventories or receivables and payables.

Profits are calculated taking into account accruals, prepayments, inventories and receivables and payables.

You should also be able to calculate the effect that a transaction will have on the cash balances of a business and on the profits of the same business.

Knowledge check 22

Cao is in business as a sole trader. His profit for the year in relation to his turnover is 18%. Explain whether or not this is a good result.

- Ratio analysis is a valuable way of analysing the performance of a business.
- It allows the comparison of the performance of different businesses. To be more meaningful the business should be in the same business sector.
- The analysis is also used to make judgements about future performance.
- It is difficult to make 'like with like' comparisons but it is regarded as the best measure that is available.
- When undertaking a ratio analysis question remember to:

  - state the formula you are using;
  - do the calculation carefully;
    state whether your result is 'better' or 'worse' than the data it is compared with;
  - give any likely reasons for your conclusion.
- Cash is money and measurement in monetary terms is objective. Profits are based using the accruals concept and the use of certain pieces of information can be subjective, e.g. provisions.

Budgeting and budgetary control

A budget is a short-term financial plan. The functions of budgeting are:
- **Planning.** They show what managers hope to achieve in the future. They show overall plans as well as departmental plans.
- **Coordinating.** Individual departments' budgets depend on each other and influence each other. They should be complementary and not contradict or conflict with each other.
- **Communicating.** Since departments are interdependent, managers and staff must communicate with each other when preparing budgets. Managers must also communicate plans to staff and to more senior managers.
- **Decision making.** Forecasting means that decisions must be made regarding sales, production etc.
- **Controlling.** Budgets must be compared with actual results. Action can then take place to eradicate problems or to replicate good practice.

Budgetary control uses budgets to manage the performance of departments in a business in order to control the performance of the business as a whole. Financial planning is delegated to managers. Their actual performance is continuously compared with those set in the budgets. This ensures that all departmental decisions and actions are in line with the corporate plans.

A **master budget** draws together all the individual departmental budgets. It is a sum of all the individual budgets and makes up a budgeted income statement and a budgeted statement of financial position.

You must also be aware that budgeting does have its limitations:
- Budgets are only as good as the data being used to draw them up.
- They may become an over-riding goal and so lead to unhealthy departmental competition and a misuse of resources. This may lead to incorrect decisions being made.

Knowledge check 23

Identify two benefits that managers would wish to gain from a system of budgeting.

Knowledge check 24

Explain the term 'budgetary control'.

Knowledge check 25

Outline one limitation of using a system of budgeting.

Examiner tip

Always show each month of a budget separately. Do not show the total of several months together. Cash budgets include bank transactions, so it is possible to have negative monthly balances in a cash budget.

Examiner tip

In your headings include the word 'budgeted' or 'forecast', and the time period covered.

Examiner tip

Show separate monthly data when preparing individual budgets. But *do not* show separate monthly data when preparing any parts of a master budget.

- Budgets might act as a demotivating factor if they are imposed by senior managers rather than being negotiated with staff.
- They may be based on easily achieved goals, so making departmental managers appear to be more efficient than they are. Easily achieved goals may also lead to complacency and underachievement.

You must be able to prepare a cash budget. Learn one layout (there are several layouts commonly used); choose a layout that you are comfortable with. Note that some business studies textbooks refer to cash budgets as cash flow forecasts.

Only cash and bank receipts and payments are included. The budget will not include any non-cash items, such as provision for depreciation or provision for doubtful debts.

The main problem occurs when either receivables and/or payables pay and are paid some months after the credit sale and/or credit purchases have taken place. You may find it easier to visualise if you imagine that all the monthly transactions have taken place on one day in the month.

Example:

Budgeted credit sales for April amount to £18 000. Half of all trade receivables will take one month's credit; the remainder will pay the following month.

If you find this confusing, imagine all the sales (£18 000) took place on 15 April. Half will pay on 15 May and half on 15 June. So, £9000 will be received in May and £9000 will be received in June.

Summary

- Budgets are an important management tool. They are short-term plans expressed in money.
- Individual budgets are summarised in a master budget.
- Cash budgets are the most popular type examined.
- Cash budgets are prepared on a cash basis and should show each set of monthly data separately. Remember that cash budgets may include information regarding future business bank transactions. So your results could end with an overdraft in one or more months. Non-cash items

(e.g. provisions for depreciation and doubtful debts) are not included.

- Budgetary control uses budgets to plan and control departmental management.
- Examination questions regarding the preparation of budgeted income statements often have a 'time lapse' included. The cash received from credit sales and the cash paid for goods supplied on credit need to be adjusted in order to find the actual purchases and sales for the income statement of the budgeted period.

Impact of ICT in accounting

Answers to this topic area tend to be either very good or very poor. It is important that you focus on the question set. Most students are very familiar with computers and what they can achieve. However, there are a couple of major pitfalls:

- Answering the question from the wrong viewpoint, for example discussing the impact that ICT will have on the business when the question asked for the impact on the workforce.

- Lack of development after a point has been identified, for example identifying that computers generally speed up record keeping but failing to explain how this happens. Try to imagine that you are explaining the answer to someone who knows nothing of computing.

You must be aware of the application of ICT in the double-entry system, and in maintaining inventory records and credit control. You must also be aware of the advantages and disadvantages of using ICT generally, and also in specific applications such as maintenance of a sales ledger, or keeping inventory records.

The main advantages of using computers in accounting are:

- The ability to process data much more quickly than is possible with manual methods, for example data concerning a credit sale need to be input only once. From this one input an invoice will be created, the entries will be made in the sales ledger and in the general ledger accounts and also inventory records will be updated.
- Very accurate entries are produced provided the initial entry is keyed in accurately.
- Large amounts of data can be handled by each operator — manually this might require many more personnel.
- Financial and statistical information is readily available in a form most suitable to the user.
- Exceptional reports are easily compiled. Programs can be adapted to report items that fall outside set parameters.

The disadvantages of using computers in accounting are mainly cost related:

- The cost of hardware and software can be high.
- Staff may need training, which can also be costly.
- Modification of software design may be costly.
- Staff may be resistant to change if they are not already familiar with using ICT.

Examiner tip

Concentrate on the question set by the examiner. Underline the points that you believe are the important parts of the question. Make sure you cover these points in your plan. This should ensure that you do not repeat yourself and that you stick to the question.

Summary

- Many students have a great deal of knowledge of ICT. They often stray from the point of the question set by the examiner.
- Make a plan and do not deviate from it.
- Be aware of the advantages that computers can bring to repetitive tasks and how they can 'multitask' easily and rapidly.
- The major disadvantages are cost related.
- Be aware of staffing implications and the effect on people who lack confidence in the use of technology.

Questions & Answers

In this section of the guide there are ten questions. Each question is followed by two sample answers interspersed with comments from the examiner.

The questions are typical of those you could be faced with in your AS examination. They are based on the format of the AS examination papers. The usual pattern is that the first part of the question will test your ability to solve a numerical problem using knowledge, understanding and application skills. The second part of the question generally involves some analysis and then an evaluation of a scenario.

Sample answers

In each case, the first answer (by Student A) is intended to show the type of response that would earn a grade A. Remember that a grade-A response does not mean that the answer is perfect. You will see that there is a range of marks that could score a grade A.

The answers given by Student B illustrate the types of error that weaker students tend to make and so deprive themselves of vital marks that could so easily have moved their script up into another grade boundary.

Resist the temptation to look at the answers before you try to answer the question.

Examiner comments

Examiner comments on the questions are preceded by the icon ⓔ. They offer tips on what you need to do to gain full marks.

Examiner comments on student answers are preceded by the icon ⓔ. In some cases they are shown within the student's answer, but in the main they appear after the student's answer. In weaker answers, the comments point out areas for improvement and the types of common error found in answers that are around the pass/fail boundary.

Assessment

Remember that the course is designed to allow you to show your ability and to use your skills. AS, as well as A2, papers assess the following assessment objectives within the context of the specification content and skills. The following assessment objectives are tested in all examination papers to varying degrees:

- **knowledge and understanding** of the accounting principles, concepts and techniques within familiar and unfamiliar situations
- **application** of knowledge and understanding to familiar and unfamiliar situations
- **analysis and evaluation** by ordering, interpreting and analysing information using an appropriate format — making judgements, decisions and recommendations after assessing alternative courses of action

Quality of written communication (QWC)

On each paper, 4 marks are awarded for the quality of written communication. The marks are split equally between written communication (for prose answers) and quality of presentation (for numerical answers). These marks are awarded in specific questions that are clearly identified on the examination paper.

The specification requires that students use:
- text that is legible, and that your spelling, punctuation and grammar ensure that the meaning is clear
- a form and style of writing that is appropriate to the purpose and to the complex subject matter
- information in a clear and coherent way, and that specialist vocabulary is used where appropriate

Unit 2

The approximate weightings for Unit 2 are:

Knowledge and understanding	20%	17 marks
Application	50%	36 marks
Analysis and evaluation	30%	23 marks
	100%	76 marks (plus 4 marks for QWC)

There are fewer marks in Unit 2 for knowledge and understanding and application than there are in Unit 1, and three times as many for the higher-level skills of analysis and evaluation.

You can learn to recognise the marks allocated to the skills of analysis and evaluation by the use of certain 'trigger' words. The most common trigger words are:
- **Advise** — suggest solutions to a problem and justify your solution.
- **Analyse** — identify the characteristics of the information given.
- **Assess** — make an informed judgement based on information supplied in the question.
- **Discuss** — present advantages and disadvantages or strengths and weaknesses of a particular line of action and arrive at a conclusion based on the question scenario.
- **To what extent** — similar to 'discuss' but requiring a judgement based on the likelihood of the potential outcomes and effects on the given scenario.

It is important that answers requiring analysis and evaluation result in a judgement being made. You use these skills almost every day. How often do you discuss with friends which cinema to visit? The whole group of friends will justify their choice to the whole group (making their judgement known).

Question I **Types of business ownership**

Harold currently works for Gloria in her general store. Gloria wishes to retire and Harold has agreed to purchase her business as a going concern.

He is unsure whether he should

(i)   trade as a sole trader, or

(ii) enter into partnership, or

(iii) make the business a private limited company

REQUIRED

Advise Harold on the type of ownership that should be adopted when he sets up in business.   (10 marks)

plus 2 marks for quality of written communication

e This is a popular type of question with examiners. It tests a student's knowledge of each type of business organisation. The word 'advise' requires a judgement to be made and is therefore testing the higher-order skill of evaluation. Students must always draw written answers to a clear conclusion when analysis and evaluative trigger words are used in a question.

Student A

There are many advantages in trading as a sole trader. Harold will be his own boss and so he can make all the business decisions without consulting anyone else. It means that he can keep all the profit earned in the business and he does not have to show anyone else his financial statements.

e This is a good start, showing that the student appreciates the advantages of trading as a sole trader.

However, there are a number of disadvantages. These include: Will he be able to cope? At the moment he is working only in the store — has he got the necessary management skills to actually be in charge of the whole business?

e This is a perceptive point that few students would comment upon.

He will have no one to discuss action plans or decisions with and to offload any business problems that he might encounter. He will have no one to cover him if he were ill or needed a day off work. Harold must stand all losses that the business might suffer and he will have unlimited liability.

e There are two good points here. An explanation of the concept of unlimited liability would have indicated that the student had not merely 'lifted' the phrase from a textbook.

The advantages to being in partnership are:

- Harold can share his action plans with other owners of the business. This could mean less stress for him. He will have cover if he is ill or on holiday.
- If the business makes a loss this will be shared between himself and the other partners.
- Probably the greatest benefit is that being in partnership will give the business access to more capital than it would if he were a sole trader.

The disadvantages of being in partnership are:

- Profits have to be shared with the other partners.
- Harold might find it stressful having to discuss all business decisions with his fellow partners.
- The biggest disadvantage is that he has unlimited liability, which extends to his fellow partners. He and his fellow partners are jointly and severally responsible for each other's business debts. He could lose his private assets because of the actions of one or other of his partners.

ⓔ This is a good section, especially the comments on unlimited liability and the development regarding the partners' responsibilities towards each other.

The advantages of becoming a private limited company are:

- Harold would have limited liability.
- He would have the kudos of being able to say that he was a director of a limited company.
- Harold could raise extra capital by selling more shares.
- He could remain in control if he made sure that any shares he sold were less in total than the shares he retained for himself.

ⓔ These are also good points, although the student could have developed the points further, especially the comment on limited liability.

The disadvantages of forming a limited company are:

- There is more red tape involved.
- Harold could lose control if other people get more shares than he has.
- Other people can look at his financial statements at Companies House.

ⓔ There are some valid points but they all lack development. What does the student mean by 'more red tape'?

Harold should form a private limited company; because of limited liability his investment is safer than the other two options, which are riskier.

ⓔ The student gives advice and justifies the choice.

ⓔ 12/12 marks awarded Overall, this is an A-grade response. The student scores maximum marks for content. Most of the usual points are covered and generally they are well developed. The main concern is the amount of material given in the answer for only 10 marks. The opportunity cost of such a detailed answer must be a cause for concern. You should allow 45 seconds per mark available, so in this case around 7½ minutes should be allocated to writing the answer.

The answer is clearly laid out and structured well. This has two benefits: it helps students to avoid repeating points and it helps examiners when there are maximum marks for each section of a complex answer.

The quality of written communication is good and the points are laid out logically, so both marks are awarded. However, there is a danger, when using a bullet point approach to an answer, that points will not be developed fully.

Student B

Harold would be his own boss if he became a sole trader; this would not be the case if he became a partner in a partnership or a limited company. All the profits would be his.

ⓔ This is a rather confused start. The student refers to partners in both a partnership and a limited company. Is this careless or confused? It is not clear under which form of business 'all the profits would be his'.

If Harold was to become bankrupt he could lose his house and his car as they would take them to settle all his debts.

ⓔ Lack of clarity means that marks cannot be rewarded in this paragraph. 'They' would take the assets — who are 'they'?

If he was a partner he could share his problems with the others. He would have to make sure that he got on with the other directors. He could have arguments with them about what the business should do. Harold will also have limited liability.

ⓔ This is confused writing once more ('the other directors in a partnership'). Harold would have unlimited liability in a partnership.

As a limited company Harold could raise more capital by selling shares but only to his family and friends but he could not lose his car and house if he went bust.

ⓔ There are two reasonable points here. The second point could have been developed to explain why he could not lose his personal assets.

ⓔ 5/12 marks awarded This answer would be a marginal fail, scoring only 4 marks. The quality of written communication scores 1 mark. A more structured approach would make the answer clearer.

Question 2 **Accounting concepts**

Tom is a sole trader. He owns a successful electronics business.

His draft income statement for the year ended 31 December 2012 reveals:

	£
Gross profit	597 650
Profit for the year	248 750

Additional information

(1) The business started trading in 1987. Since then sales have increased by 400% and the number of customers has more than doubled. The business has an extremely good name in the trade. As a result Tom has introduced £100 000 goodwill into his statement of financial position at 31 December 2012. His bookkeeping entries were:

	Debit	Credit
	£	£
Goodwill	100 000	
Profit and loss section of income statement		100 000

(2) Tom has been negotiating with the bursar of a local college to supply the college with office equipment. He feels certain that a contract for the equipment worth £120 000 will be signed in mid-January 2013. He has included £120 000 as sales for the year ended 31 December 2012.

(3) Tom purchased his premises in 1987 for £80 000. The market value of the premises fell between 1987 and 2007. Consequently, Tom depreciated his premises at 2% per annum until 31 December 2007. Since then property prices in the area have started to rise. Because of this, Tom has not provided for depreciation on premises in the income statement for the year ended 31 December 2012.

(4) Tom valued his inventory for the year ended 31 December 2012 at cost, £60 000. Included in this figure are six microwave cookers that have been damaged. They cost £30 each. After repairing the microwaves at a total cost of £100 they could all be sold for £250.

(5) Tom has included in the income statement for the year ended 31 December 2012, as motor expenses, a new car costing £12 000 purchased as a birthday present for his wife. 'She helps me a lot in the business so she deserves it,' he says.

REQUIRED

(a) Explain how each item should be treated in financial statements, making reference to generally accepted accounting concepts.   (15 marks)

(b) Calculate, for the year ended 31 December 2012:
   (i) the corrected gross profit
   (ii) the corrected profit for the year   (9 marks)

 Students must ensure that they fully understand the basic accounting concepts since they are fundamental to the preparation of all financial statements. The question tests students' understanding of the theory underlying each concept and also tests their ability to apply each concept to a set of financial statements. In part (b) students must respond to each scenario even when there is no change to the statements.

> ### Student A
>
> **(a)** **(1)** Incorrect. Tom can only include goodwill in his accounts if he purchased it from another business. He can't add it into his income statement because it is not profit from his usual sales of electronic goods.
> Prudence concept.

 **3/3 marks awarded** This is a clear answer that scores the maximum marks.

> **(2)** Incorrect. The sales must be included in next year's income statement because Tom cannot be certain that the college will complete the deal next year.
> Prudence concept.

 **3/3 marks awarded** Another good answer. The realisation concept is also an acceptable response. This states that a sale is not recognised until the title to the goods passes to the customer, or until the goods are exchanged for cash or an asset (i.e. a trade receivable). Neither of these conditions will be satisfied until January 2013 if the deal goes ahead.

> **(3)** Depreciation is not the drop in value of an asset. It is the apportioning of the cost of the premises over the time the premises will be used — the accruals concept. Tom cannot stop depreciation in the future, he would be going against the concept of consistency. So he must keep charging 2% depreciation on his premises otherwise it would make it difficult to compare the results shown in his accounts with the results from previous years' accounts.

 **3/3 marks awarded** The student gives a good definition that is summarised in the accruals concept. The student also explains the need for consistency when preparing the financial statements of a business.

> **(4)** Prudence says that inventories must be valued at either cost or net realisable value, whichever is lower. The microwaves have been valued at £180, which is what they cost originally. They should have been valued at a NBV of £150 so £30 needs to come off the inventory figure, which lowers profits by the same amount.

 **3/3 marks awarded** This is a clear answer. The only slight blemish is the use of the term 'net book value' (NBV) rather than 'net realisable value'. This is a common error in examination answers. The student does use the correct term in the original definition.

(5) Private expenditure should not be included in the income statement, it should be shown in the statement of financial position. It is drawings so profit will go up by £12 000.
      This is an example of the concept of capital expenditure.

ⓔ **2/3 marks awarded** This is a correct analysis of the transaction. However, the concept involved is the business entity concept. Purchase of a private car is not capital expenditure for the business.

(b)

(i) **Gross profit**		(ii) **Profit for the year**	
	£		£
Original gross profit	597 650	Original net profit	248 750
1) Goodwill	–		(100 000)
2) Sales	(120 000)		(120 000)
3) Depreciation	–		(1 600)
4) Stock	(30)		(30)
5) Car	–		12 000
Corrected gross profit	477 620	Corrected net profit	39 120

ⓔ **9/9 marks awarded** This excellent answer gains maximum marks. It is well laid out and labelled clearly by number and description. It is pleasing to see that the student has shown that certain items have no effect on the gross profit.

ⓔ Overall the student scores 23 marks — a clear A-grade response.

Student B

(a) (1) If sales have gone up by £400 000 and Tom has twice as many customers is £100 000 enough for goodwill? I think that £200 000 is a better figure.
      Capital expenditure.

ⓔ **0/3 marks awarded** This is a poor, subjective answer. The student has not addressed the question. You must stick to the facts as outlined in the question and not express personal opinions unless they are asked for. No marks are awarded here.

(2) If the college bursar says that they will definitely sign the contract then it is OK to include it in this year's statements since that is when Tom got to know about it being a definite sale. It's to do with the accruals concept.

ⓔ **1/3 marks awarded** The accruals concept is acceptable as an answer since realisation is a subset of the concept. However, the remainder of the response is incorrect as a sale takes place only when the title to the goods passes from the supplier. The student earns 1 mark for identifying the correct concept.

(3) He should still charge 2% depreciation so that he stays consistent. This is what the concept of consistency says.

e 2/3 marks awarded The correct concept is clearly identified and applied, earning 2 marks. The third mark could be scored by developing the answer to include the need for consistency if comparisons are to be made.

(4) Inventory has got to be valued at cost or net realisable value. They cost £180 and could be sold for £1500. The repair bill was £600. Prudence.

e 1/3 marks awarded The concept is identified correctly again, but the student does not state how inventory should be valued, i.e. is the lower or the higher value to be used? The student has not read the question carefully and has made calculations based on items selling for £250 each and repairs costing £100 per microwave. Precision in reading and answering questions is important.

(5) This is a private expense and should not be included in motor expenses. It is drawings and should be in the financed by section of the statement of financial position.

e 1/3 marks awarded The student gains a mark for stating that the new private car is not motor expenses, but development to identify the concept and the reason for the classification as drawings would score further marks.

e Part (a) scores 5 marks.

(b)	597 650
	(180)
	1 500
	12 000
	610 970
	248 750
	(1 600)
	(180)
	1 500
	(600)
	12 000
	259 870

e 3/9 marks awarded Lack of labels makes this answer difficult to mark. It is unclear whether the student does not know how to cope with the goodwill or the potential college sale. If the student did leave these two items out deliberately, this should be indicated in the answer (as Student A did). The student scores marks in the profit for the year calculation: 1 mark for depreciation, 1 mark for the vehicle adjustment and 1 mark for an own figure total. The own figure total mark cannot be rewarded in the gross profit calculation because the total is affected by the inclusion of the vehicle.

e Overall, the student scores 8 marks — insufficient for a pass grade.

Question 3 Preparing income statements and statements of financial position of sole traders

This is a long question and can be used as a 'one question test'. The length of it means that it could form two questions in a mock examination or in an actual AS examination.

The following trial balance has been extracted from the books of account of Arun Kumar.

Trial balance at 30 November 2012

	Debit	Credit
	£	£
Bad debts	500	
Bank balance	1 825	
Capital		12 971
Carriage inwards	650	
Carriage outwards	2 798	
Commission received		2 600
Discounts	1 280	
Drawings	32 700	
General expenses	37 981	
Lighting and heating expenses	9 824	
Motor expenses	15 619	
Motor van at cost	40 000	
Office equipment at cost	24 000	
Provisions for depreciation — office equipment		14 400
— motor van		17 500
Provision for doubtful debts		1 400
Purchases and sales	212 477	432 728
Rent	8 000	
Returns	1 278	934
Inventory at 1 December 2011	23 720	
Telephone	6 481	
Trade receivables and trade payables	30 000	27 080
Wages	60 480	
	509 613	509 613

Additional information at 30 November 2012

(1) Inventory was valued at £26 418.

(2) Wages owing amounted to £1760.

(3) Commission receivable owing amounted to £200.

(4) Telephone rental paid in advance amounted to £100.

(5) Provision for doubtful debts is to be maintained at 5% of trade receivables outstanding at the year end.

(6) Depreciation is to be provided at the following rates:
- **Office equipment at 10% per annum using the straight-line method**
- **Motor van at 25% per annum using the reducing balance method**

REQUIRED

(a) Prepare an income statement for the year ended 30 November 2012.

(29 marks)

plus 1 mark for quality of presentation

(b) Prepare a statement of financial position at 30 November 2012

(14 marks)

plus 1 mark for quality of presentation

(e) As already indicated, this is a big question that would in all probability take the form of two separate questions in an examination. First, it tests a student's ability to prepare an income statement. The data given in the trial balance has to be amended to take into account almost every possible adjustment that the specification allows. Second, students are required to prepare a statement of financial position that incorporates adjustments made to the income statement.

The question requires the two statements to be prepared in good style and format if the two 'quality' marks are to be gained. Students should regard the 'quality' marks as being important since these are marks that are generally easily gained and could make the difference between one grade and another.

Student A

(a)   **A. Kumar. Income statement for the year ended 30 November 2012**

	£	£
Sales		431 450
Less cost of sales		
Inventory	23 720	
Purchases	212 193	
	235 913	
Inventory	26 418	209 495
Gross profit		221 955
Less expenses		
Commission	2 800	
Carriage inwards	650	
Discounts	1 280	
Motor expenses	15 619	
Wages	62 240	
Rent	8 000	
Bad debts	500	

	£	£
Provision for doubtful debts	100	
General expenses	37981	
Telephone	6381	
Light and heat	9824	
Depreciation — office equipment	2400	
Depreciation — van	5625	153400
Profit		68555

ⓔ **24/30 marks awarded** This is a good answer, scoring 23 marks for content. The student fails to show workings, which can prove disastrous if the more complicated figures are incorrect. For example, the figure used for purchases might have scored, but the examiner cannot tell how '£212 193' has been calculated. Had workings been shown for commission, the student would score a further 2 marks — 1 mark for £2600, another mark for £200 — the only penalty being the resulting total, which should be added to the gross profit. Carriage outwards is missing and carriage inwards appears in the income statement. The extraneous item in the expenses also contaminates the profit for the year. The quality of presentation mark is scored: the heading is perfect as are the descriptors of each profit figure, and the cost of sales figure is identified.

(b)   **A. Kumar. Statement of financial position at 30 November 2012**

	£	£	£
Non-current assets			
Office equipment		24000	
Depreciation		16800	7200
Motor vehicle		40000	
Depreciation		23125	16875
Current assets			
Inventory		26418	
Receivables	30000		
Prov DD	1500	28500	
Bank		1825	
Commission received		200	
Telephone		100	
		57043	
Current liabilities			
Payables	27080		
Wages	1760	28840	28203
			52278
Capital			12971

	£	£	£
Profit			68555
			81526
Drawings			32700
			48826

(e) **15/15 marks awarded** This is a good statement of financial position that scores maximum marks. The presentation is good, earning the mark for the heading and the categorising of the components into non-current and current assets, current liabilities and capital. The student should have shown a total for non-current assets, but this is only a minor omission. Although the statement of financial position does not balance, all the figures are correct (including the profit using the student's own figure).

(e) The student scores 39 out of 45 marks: a grade-A answer.

(a)

A. Kumar. I S y/e 30/11/12

	£	£
Sales		432728
Returns		934
		431794
Inventory	23720	
Purchases	212477	
Returns	1278	
Inventory	26418	208501
G P		223293
Commission received (2600 – 200)		2400
G P		225693
Carriage in		650
Carriage out		2798
Motor expenses		15619
Wages (60 480 + 1760)		62240
Rent		8000
Bad debts		500
Provision doubtful debts (1400 × 5%)		7000
General expenses		37981
Light and heat		9824
Telephone		6481
Office equipment depr (40000 × 25%)		10000
Van depr (17500 × 25%)		4375
		165468
		60225

e **15/30 marks awarded** This is a curious mixture of an answer. The good point is that the student provided workings, shown in italics. This means that some marks are scored for commission received, telephone and depreciation on the van. The weaker points are in the general layout, which is confused. The presentation mark cannot be awarded for several reasons: profit for the year is not identified, the term 'gross profit' is abbreviated to 'GP' and the heading for the income statement contains many abbreviations. Carriage inwards is an extraneous item and, even if the profit for the year had been identified, the contamination of the expenses total would have resulted in the loss of this mark. The student scores 15 marks out of 30, mainly because of workings.

(b)   **Statement of financial position**

NCA			
Office equipment	24000		
Depreciation	10000	14000	
Van	40000		
Depreciation	4375	35625	
CA Inventory	26418		
Recs	30000		
Bank	1825		
Telephone	100		
	58343		
CL			
Pays	30000		
Wages	1760		
Comm	200	26383	
		62008	
Capital		12971	
Profit		60225	
		73196	
Drawings		32700	
		105896	

e **8/15 marks awarded** Some careless, basic errors cost the student valuable marks here. The statement of financial position heading should contain the date and the sections must be clearly marked as 'Non-current assets', 'Current assets' etc. so no mark is awarded for quality of presentation. The student uses only the current year's depreciation for both non-current assets rather than the aggregate depreciation figure. The provision for doubtful debts is not deducted from the receivables figure. Commission owed at the end of the year is mistakenly treated as a current liability. Other careless errors are the use of the receivables amount as payables, and drawings being added to the capital figure.

e Overall, the student scores 23 marks for a standard question — insufficient for a pass grade.

Question 4 **Presentation of income statements and statements of financial position of sole traders**

This is a long question and can be used as a 'one question test'. The length of it means that it could form two questions in a mock examination or in an actual AS examination.

Jacques Lefevre provides the following information.

Trial balance at 29 February 2012

	Debit	Credit
	£	£
Bad debts	450	
Bad debts recovered		125
Bank balance		6320
Capital		60118
Carriage inwards	312	
Carriage outwards	840	
Cash in hand	420	
Discounts	216	114
Drawings	24000	
Equipment at cost	20000	
General expenses	14720	
Light and heating expenses	4310	
Machinery at cost	50000	
Provision for doubtful debts		350
Provisions for depreciation — Equipment		12800
— Machinery		6500
Purchases and sales	45892	99346
Rent receivable		4800
Returns	542	722
Inventory 1 March 2011	6473	
Telephone	2470	
Trade receivables and trade payables	10400	6250
Wages	16400	16400
	197445	197445

Additional information at 28 February 2012

(1) Inventory was valued at £5139.

(2) Wages paid in advance amounted to £412.

(3) Rent receivable in advance £500.

(4) Heating bill due but not yet paid £175.

(5) Provision for doubtful debts is to be maintained at 3% of trade receivables outstanding at the year end.

(6) Jacques provides depreciation at the following rates:
- **machinery — 10% using the straight-line method**
- **equipment — 40% using the reducing balance method**

(7) Jacques took goods valued at £200 from the business for his personal use.

REQUIRED

Prepare:

(a) an income statement for the year ended 29 February 2012   (30 marks)

plus 1 mark for quality of presentation

(b) a statement of financial position at 29 February 2012   (15 marks)

plus 1 mark for quality of presentation

ⓔ Another 'long' question that requires concentration on the application of the accruals concept. Once more there are 'quality' marks available so students must concentrate on good presentation of each statement. All headings should be written in full, avoiding abbreviations, and workings should be shown when taking into account the necessary adjustments.

Student A

(a)   J. Lefevre. Income statement for the year ended 29 February 2012

	£	£
Sales		99 346
Returns in		542
		98 804
Less cost of sales		
Inventory	6 473	
Purchases	45 692	
Carriage inwards	312	
Returns out	(722)	
Inventory	(5 139)	46 616
Gross profit		52 188
Rent received		4 300
Provision for doubtful debts		38
Discount received		114
		56 640
Less expenses		
Wages	15 988	
Bad debts	575	
Carriage out	840	
Light and heat	4 485	

	£	£
Telephone	2470	
Gen expenses	14720	
Discount allowed	216	
Depn — Machinery	5000	
— Equipment	2880	47174
Profit		9466

🅔 **29/31 marks awarded** This is an excellent answer. However, the student does not show any workings. This can be dangerous since, if any of the figures in the financial statements do not agree with the figures shown in the examiner's mark scheme, no marks can be awarded.

Student A could have scored 1 extra mark for showing workings for bad debts. Remember, it could be 1 mark that moves your grade up. The layout is good and is rewarded with the appropriate mark. The exception is the trading section layout; a more conventional layout would be better. The labelling is clear and accurate. This answer scores 28 out of 30 content marks.

(b) **Statement of financial position at 29 February 2012**

	£	£	£
Non-current assets			
Machinery		50000	
Depreciation		11500	38500
Equipment		20000	
Depreciation		15680	4320
			42820
Current assets			
Inventory		5139	
Receivables	10400		
Provision for doubtful debts	312	10088	
Bank balance		6320	
Cash		420	
Prepayment		412	
		22379	
Current liabilities			
Payables	6250		
Accrued expenses	175		
Rent rec	500	6925	15454
			58274
Capital			60118
Add profit			9466
			69584
Drawings			24200
			45384

e **15/16 marks awarded** This is a good statement of financial position, neatly presented and labelled accurately and well. The statement of financial position scores the quality of presentation mark despite the fact that it does not balance. Remember, if an account or statement does not balance, all is not lost. Quickly check that you have not missed an item from the information given. Check that you have double-entered all the additional information. If these two checks do not reveal your error, move on and tackle the next question. If you have any spare time at the end of your examination, you can revisit the question and conduct a more thorough search for your error(s). Remember, an answer does not have to be perfect to score a pass mark. This student drops only 1 mark; in the panic of the examination room he/she has not realised that the bank balance is a credit entry in the trial balance and includes it incorrectly as a current asset.

e Overall, the student gives a grade-A answer — 44/47 marks.

Student B

(a)

Income statement at 29 February 2012

	£	£	£	
Sales			99 346	
Returns			542	
			98 804	
Inventory		6 473		
Purchases	45 892			
Returns	722	45 170		
		51 643		
Inventory		4 939		
Cost of goods sold			46 704	
Gross profit			52 100	
Rent received (4800 + 500)		5 300		
Wages (16 400 – 412)		15 988		
Carriages		1 152		
Light and heat (4310 + 175)		4 485		
Telephone		2 470		
Gen expenses		14 720		
Discount		102		
Prov doubtful debts (350 – 312)		38		
Machinery	50 000			
Depn	5 000	45 000		(50 000 x 10%)
Equip	20 000			(20 000 x 40%)
Depn	8 000	12 000	101 255	
Loss			49 155	

e **16/31 marks awarded** Student B does not score the quality of presentation mark, as the heading does not contain the business name and should also state that the statement is for the year ended 29 February 2012. Although there are many errors, the student scores 16 marks. Errors include the deduction of goods for own use from the closing inventory, and the inclusion of an incorrect figure for rent received as an expense rather than as an addition to the gross profit.

The student shows good workings to support the figures used in the income statement. The loss does not score since the expenses are corrupted by two extraneous items — the two non-current assets. However, 1 mark is awarded for each calculation of the depreciation figures.

(b)

Statement of financial position at 29 February

	£	£	£
Non-current assets			
Machinery		50 000	
Depreciation		11 500	38 500
Equipment		20 000	
Depreciation		20 800	?
Current assets			
Inventory		4 939	
Receivables	10 400		
Provision	38	10 362	
Cash		420	
Wages		412	
Rent		500	
		16 633	
Current liabilities			
Payables	6 250		
Bank o/d	6 320		
Heating	175	12 745	3 988
		Total should be 13 037	
		mistake somewhere	
Capital			60 118
Less loss			49 155
			10 963
Drawings			24 000
			13 037

ⓔ **12/16 marks awarded** Despite making a few mistakes, Student B scores 12 marks, including the mark for presentation. Three marks are scored for each of the non-current assets, current assets and current liabilities. Something has gone wrong with the depreciation of machinery and the student realises this (hence the question mark). Rent received is treated as a current asset rather than as a current liability.

Student B kindly points out that the statement of financial position does not balance. Do not be tempted to do this or to include a suspense item. This wastes time that could more profitably be spent on gaining marks elsewhere. The drawings figure should have included the drawings of goods.

ⓔ Overall, this student earns 28 marks — a low pass grade.

Question 5 **Preparing entries in ledger accounts for adjustments**

Olaf Svennsen provides the following information:

Trial balance at 31 December 2012

	Debit	Credit
	£	£
Balance at bank	3 127	
Capital at 1 January 2012		62 886
Delivery van at cost	40 000	
Drawings	18 400	
General expenses	18 526	
Office equipment at cost	24 000	
Provision for depreciation		
Delivery vehicle		19 520
Office equipment		14 400
Purchases and sales	97 461	163 744
Rent and rates	4 920	
Inventory at 1 January 2012	9 872	
Trade payables		4 927
Trade receivables	6 388	
Wages	42 783	
	265 477	265 477

Additional information at 31 December 2012

(1) Inventory was valued at £10 726.

(2) Olaf has withdrawn goods from the business valued at £210 for his private use during the year.

(3) Wages due and unpaid amounted to £899.

(4) Rates paid in advance amounted to £1300.

(5) Depreciation is provided on the delivery vehicle at 20% per annum using the reducing balance method.

(6) Depreciation is provided on office equipment at 10% per annum using the straight-line method.

REQUIRED

(a) Prepare:
  (i) a wages account
  (ii) a rent and rates account
  (iii) a provision for depreciation of delivery vehicles at cost account

(Note: Start with the balances shown in the trial balance and show clearly any transfers to other accounts.) (12 marks)

(b) Prepare an income statement for the year ended 31 December 2012 and a statement of financial position at that date. (30 marks)

(c) Discuss reasons why a trader provides for depreciation on non-current assets. (6 marks)

plus 2 marks for quality of written communication

ⓔ This question links AS Unit 1 and AS Unit 2 by including accruals and prepayments into ledger accounts. Students need to take care entering debit balances and credit balances at the end of an accounting period. A common error is to include the balances 'inside' the account rather than after the account has been closed. In this type of question the accounts that have been prepared can be used as 'working papers' providing information for the financial statements. The discussion part of the question needs to reach a conclusion to gain maximum marks.

Student A

(a)

Wages account

Balance b/d	42 783	Income statement	43 682
Balance c/d	899		
	43 682		43 682
		Balance b/d	899

Rent and rates account

Balance b/d	4 920	In st	3 620
		Balance b/d	1 300
	4 920		4 920
Balance b/d	1 300		

Depreciation of delivery vehicle account

		Balance b/d	19 520
Bal c/d	23 616	Inc stat	4 096
	23 616		23 616
		Balance b/d	23 616

ⓔ **12/12 marks awarded** This is an almost perfect answer. It has been accurately prepared. In this case, abbreviations are acceptable, because the accounts produced are part of the working papers used to arrive at the figures to be used in the financial statements. However, in order to avoid confusion about when abbreviations are acceptable, you are advised to avoid their use in all answers. The wages account is a good example of how to prepare an account in the general ledger.

(b)   O. Svennsen. Income statement for the year ended 31 December 2012

	£	£	£
Sales			163 744
Less cost of sales			
Inventory		9 872	
Purchases	97 461		
Goods own use	210	97 251	
		107 123	
Inventory		10 726	96 397
Gross profit			67 347
Less expenses			
Wages (42 783 + 899)		43 682	
Rent and rates (4920 – 1300)		3 620	
General expenses		18 526	
Depn — office equipment	2 400		
Depn — vehicle (20 480 × 20%)	4 096	6 496	72 324
Loss			4 977

ⓔ This good answer scores maximum marks. However, the student may have used up valuable time in showing the workings; the figure to be used had already been calculated in the ledger accounts in part (a) of the answer. These are their 'working papers' for this question.

Statement of financial position at 31 December 2012

	£	£	£
Non-current assets			
Office equipment		24 000	
Depreciation		16 800	7 200
Delivery vehicle at cost		40 000	
Depreciation		23 616	16 384
			23 584
Current assets			
Inventory		10 726	
Trade receivables		6 388	
Bank		3 127	
Prepayment		1 300	
		21 541	
Current liabilities			
Payables	4 927		
Accruals	899	5 826	15 715
			39 299

	£	£	£
Capital			62 866
Loss			4 977
			57 909
Drawings			18 610
			39 256

ⓔ This is a well-presented statement of financial position, accurately prepared, with all assets and liabilities classified correctly. Notice the excellent use of inset figures to aid the calculation of relevant sub-totals.

ⓔ **30/30 marks awarded for part (b)**

(c) Depreciation is the spreading of the cost into each income statement for as long as the non-current asset is owned in the business. We have to put depreciation into the income statement each year the asset is used. This is because of the matching concept. We are using the asset to produce our goods so we must charge part of the asset with all the other expenses. We should always be consistent in calculating the depreciation otherwise we cannot compare sets of statements. If you start using the straight-line method you must continue to use it.

Conclusion. We must depreciate all non-current assets but not land. So that we are being consistent and the financial statements will then give a true and fair view.

ⓔ **8/8 marks awarded** This good answer covers all the necessary points, scoring maximum marks. There are good references to the matching concept and the concept of consistency, and some good developments. Student A has given a conclusion. Questions asking for a discussion either require a conclusion or the points must be brought together with a judgement. Although not written in perfect English, the text is clear and the student has communicated well. Student A scores 6 marks for content and 2 marks for written communication.

ⓔ Overall, the student earns 50 marks — a grade-A answer.

Student B

(a)

Wages			
Trial balance	42 783	Balancing figure	41 884
		Balance c/d	899
	42 783		42 783

Rent and rates			
Trial balance	4 920	Balancing figure	6 220
Balance c/d	1 300		
	6 220		6 220

Depreciation			
		Trial balance	19 520
Balance c/d	23 616	Depreciation	4 096
	23 616		23 616

e **4/12 marks awarded** Student B has made a common error by placing the debit and credit balances for accrued expenses and prepayments in the accounts as opening balances rather than after the accounts have been balanced. It is safer to enter the credit for wages under the account as a credit balance and then bring it back up into the account. Similarly, with the rates prepayment, enter it as a debit under the account and bring it back up into the account as a credit entry. This technique also ensures that all balances are brought down. All accounts in the general ledger should state the word 'account' after the description, e.g. 'wages account'.

Three marks are awarded for the opening entries in each account. The transfers to the income statement in the wages and rent and rates accounts do not score because they are inappropriately described, although the entry for depreciation £4096 is given a 'benefit of the doubt' mark.

(b)

Sales			163 744
Inventory		9 872	
Purchases		97 461	
		107 333	
Inventory		10 516	96 817
Gross profit			66 927
Wages		42 783	
Rent		4 920	
General expenses		18 526	
Depreciation		6 496	72 725
⊓			94 202

e This is a careless answer. There is no heading, profit has been abbreviated as ⊓, and the expenses are greater than the gross profit, resulting in a net loss. Goods for own use have been incorrectly deducted from the closing inventory.

The student scores a total of 10 marks. They gain 3 marks in the trading section of the income statement (sales, purchases and gross profit). Each of the expenses scores a single mark and the depreciation total scores all 4 marks allocated. It would be safer to show the breakdown of the depreciation figure in case the total is incorrect.

SOFP	
Office equipment (24 000 – 6496)	17 504
Delivery van	40 000
	57 504
CA inventory	10 516
Recs	6 388
Bank	3 127
	20 031
pays	4 927
	15 104
	72 608

Capital	6 886
Profit	94 202
	101 088
Dwgs	18 400
	82 688

ⓔ **The student scores 8 out of 15 marks.** This is a confused layout. Although many of the figures are correct, a better layout would make the student's calculations (and the examiner's work) more straightforward. Insetting some of the figures would make the statement of financial position more acceptable. Headings and some descriptions are poor.

ⓔ **18/30 marks awarded for part (b)**

(c) Depreciation can be straight line or reducing balance. Straight line is much easier to do than reducing balance that can be quiet complicated especially after a few years. Reducing balance is more lifelike and it means that you have more money in the account to buy the next one. Your car depreciates more in the first couple of years than later. You have to depreciate all your assets so that you know how much they can be sold for later. You have to depreciate things because its the law so you don't have to pay to much tax or VAT.

ⓔ **0/8 marks awarded** This is a purely descriptive answer that offers little discussion. There are several grammatical and spelling errors. The student makes fundamental errors in the descriptions. Depreciation is a non-cash transaction. The carrying amount does not state how much assets can be sold for and it is not law. The student cannot be awarded any marks for this answer.

ⓔ Overall, Student B's answer earns 22 out of 50 marks and does not attain the pass criteria.

Question 6 **Capital and revenue expenditure**

Discuss the importance of classifying expenditure into capital expenditure and revenue expenditure.

(8 marks)

plus 2 marks for quality of written communication

ⓔ Another 'discuss' question; so a conclusion must be given. In written questions it is helpful for students to prepare a plan (see the answer given by Student A). A plan will not be marked by the examiner, so abbreviations and 'shorthand' that is understandable only to the writer are acceptable. The answer itself will be marked for written communication skills and so must not contain spelling mistakes or abbreviations and should be grammatically well presented.

Student A

Plan: def inc on inc stat cap on sofp if not in st wrong sofp wrong true fair

Capital expenditure is spending on non-current assets or their improvement, whereas revenue expenditure is spending on the day to day running costs of the business. An example of capital expenditure is spending on purchasing some new machinery.

Capital expenditure is always shown on the statement of financial position part of the financial statements whereas revenue expenditure is always entered in the income statement.

If capital expenditure was shown on the inc stat the profit would be too small and the non-current assets in the statement of financial position would be undervalued. This means that the financial statements would not show a true and fair view of the business.

I believe that it is very important that all spending is classified correctly otherwise all the parts of the statements are wrong. So care must be taken to get the classification right.

ⓔ **10/10 marks awarded** Maximum marks are scored for both the answer and quality of written communication. It is good to note that Student A produced a plan for the answer. This helps in all written answers since it allows students to assemble their answers in a logical way. It also avoids repetition of the same point, which often wastes time. It is also good to see the two parts of the question being compared by the simple use of the word 'whereas'. The student rounded off the discussion with a judgement: a grade-A answer.

Student B

Capital expenditure is spending on non-everyday things. It cannot be used to pay dividends but dividends can be paid out of revenue expenditure.

If a lot of dividends are paid out of revenue expenditure then profits will suffer but this is quite good because less tax will need to be paid, but if they are going to sell the business it is better not to pay dividends because the purchaser will see higher profits.

I think that you should split the capital and revenue expenditure because it says so in the IAS laws.

e **1/10 marks awarded** This poor answer contains many basic errors and earns no marks for content. Student B confuses capital and revenue expenditure with capital reserves and revenue reserves. The student also refers to taxation. This should be avoided in the vast majority of cases since taxation is a complex topic that depends on many issues, not merely the level of reported profits. Communication is quite good and scores the only mark awarded.

e Clearly, nowhere near a pass grade answer.

Question 7 **Rights issue of shares**

The following trial balance has been extracted from the books of account of **Westburn Ltd** at **31 March 2012** *after* the preparation of the income statement.

	Debit £000	Credit £000
Balance at bank	114	
8% debentures (2024)		100
Ordinary shares of £1 each fully paid		600
Property plant and equipment	930	
Provision for corporation tax		27
Retained earnings at 31 March 2012		78
Share premium account		300
Inventories	48	
Trade payables		32
Trade receivables	45	
	1 137	1 137

The following adjustments need to be made before the preparation of a statement of financial position.

(1) The directors have had the property plant and equipment revalued at £1 300 000.

(2) The directors made a rights issue of ordinary shares, at a premium of 45 pence per share, on the basis of 1 new ordinary share for every 3 shares held. The issue was fully subscribed.

REQUIRED

(a) Prepare a statement of financial position at 31 March 2012 after taking into account any necessary adjustments.

(15 marks)

plus 2 marks for quality of presentation

(b) Calculate the gearing ratio before and after making any necessary adjustments. *(3 marks)*

(c) Discuss the changes to the gearing ratio in the light of any adjustments made. *(8 marks)*

plus 2 marks for quality of written communication

ⓔ A wide-ranging question that requires a 'well presented' statement of financial position. This means good accurate headings, as well as accurately calculated adjustments. When ratios need to be calculated, students must give the formula they use. This is especially true when calculating a gearing ratio since there are a number of acceptable versions; an examiner needs to know which one the student has used. The discussion will show how well the student understands gearing.

Student A

(a)

Westburn Ltd. Statement of financial position at 31 March 2012

	£000	£000
Non-current assets		
Property plant and equipment		1300
Current assets		
Inventories	48	
Trade receivables	45	
Balance at bank	404	
	497	
Current liabilities		
Trade payables	32	
Tax liability	27	
	59	
Net current assets		438
		1738
Non-current liabilities		
8% debentures (2024)		100
		1638
Equity		
Share capital		800
Share premium account		390
Revaluation reserve		370
Retained earnings		78
		1638

🅔 **17/17 marks awarded** This is an excellent answer. It is arithmetically accurate and has excellent presentation. Workings could have been shown as an insurance against an arithmetic error. Otherwise, it is flawless.

(b) $\dfrac{\text{Debt}}{\text{Capital employed}} \times 100$

Before $\dfrac{100}{1078} \times 100 = 9.28\%$

After $\dfrac{100}{1738} \times 100 = 5.75\%$

🅔 **3/3 marks awarded** The student produces another perfect answer that is clear, well laid out and supported by workings.

(c) The gearing ratio was low before the rights issue of shares and the revaluation of property plant and equipment. Anything below 50% is considered to be low. After the changes it is now even lower. This is because the debentures have stayed the same but the shareholders' funds have increased by £290000 share premium and the revaluation reserve has gone up by £370000 — a total increase of £660000.

The company has £100000 of 8% debentures. Debentures have to be repaid in 2024 and the company must pay the holders £8000 each year whether the company makes a profit or a loss. At the moment they have £404000 in the bank so they could pay the interest more than 50 times over.

Because the company has such a small proportion of its total capital provided by outsiders (lenders) it should not have any difficulty borrowing further finance in the future should it need to.

ⓔ **10/10 marks awarded** This is an excellent answer that covers all the pertinent points. It is well expressed too, so it gains maximum marks.

ⓔ Maximum marks throughout — clearly a grade-A answer.

Student B

(a)
Statement of financial position

Non-current assets		
Property plant and equipment		1 300
Current assets		
Inventories	48	
Trade payables	32	
Balance at bank	114	
		1 494
Less current liabilities		
Trade receivables		45
		1 449
Share capital and reserves		
Ordinary shares		890
Share premium account		100
Revaluation reserve		300
Retained earnings		78
Debentures		100
		1 468

ⓔ **5/17 marks awarded** Student B scores only 1 presentation mark: the heading lacks the company name and the date of the statement of financial position. The difference between trade receivables and trade payables is confused. This student might have scored a couple of extra marks had the workings for ordinary shares and share premium been shown. Remember to back up all figures with workings — the examiner cannot see them inside your calculator. It is safer to include debentures in the top section of a statement of financial position. Wherever debentures are entered, they should be labelled as a non-current liability. It is not clear to an examiner whether this student believes that debentures are shares or reserves.

(b) Gearing ratio = $\dfrac{\text{Owings}}{\text{Shares}}$

Before $\dfrac{159}{600}$ = 0.265

After $\dfrac{145}{890}$ = 0.1629

ⓔ **0/3 marks awarded** Clearly Student B does not know how to calculate the gearing ratio. Remember there is no substitute for learning all the ratios listed in the specification. In your examination there will be questions using ratios.

(c) The gearing ratio has dropped considerably. In 2008 it was .26 but this year it is only .16. This shows that the company is in a bad way.

The big money got from revaluing and the share sale should be used to buy more non-current assets so that they can make more profits in the future.

ⓔ **0/10 marks awarded** Student B does not understand the concept of gearing or its significance to a business. There is also the misunderstanding that reserves are caches of money available to the directors for expansion or other uses. Remember that reserves are profits and are not necessarily backed by cash resources. No marks are scored.

ⓔ Overall, this answer earns 5 marks out of 50 and does not warrant a pass grade.

Question 8 **Rights and bonus issue of shares**

The summarised statement of financial position of Plugalot Ltd is shown as follows:

Plugalot Ltd. Statement of financial position at 31 March 2012

	£	£
Non-current assets		
Property plant and equipment	180 000	
Depreciation	75 000	105 000
Current assets excluding bank	34 000	
Balance at bank	1 200	35 200
		140 200
Equity		
Ordinary shares of £1 each fully paid		30 000
Share premium account		60 000
Retained earnings		50 200
		140 200

Additional information

(1) The directors of the company have had the property plant and equipment at 31 March 2012 revalued at £200 000.

(2) On 31 March the directors made a rights issue of 100 000 ordinary shares at a premium of 25 pence per share. The issue was fully subscribed on that date.

(3) Immediately after the rights issue the company issued one bonus share for every two shares held (the rights issue was eligible for the bonus issue). It is company policy to maintain reserves in their most flexible form and to use appropriate reserves equally.

REQUIRED

(a) Prepare a summarised statement of financial position at 31 March 2012 immediately after the revaluation of property plant and equipment and both share issues.   (16 marks)

(b) Discuss the differences between a rights issue and a bonus issue of shares.   (5 marks)

(c) Explain the circumstances in which a rights issue and a bonus issue might be made.   (4 marks)

ⓔ Another popular topic; many students get the two types of share issue confused. The question requires knowledge of the two issues with a development needed in part (c). The revaluation involves both the non-current asset and the aggregate depreciation. Workings are important when there are a number of adjustments. They should be shown, especially, if a calculator is being used. Note that part (b) requires a conclusion but part (c) requires only explanations.

Student A

(a)

Plugalot Ltd. Statement of financial position at 31 March 2012

Non-current assets		
Property plant and equipment		200000
Current assets	34000	
Bank	126200	160200
		360200
Equity		
Ordinary shares (100 + 30 + 65)		195000
Share premium (60 − 32.5 + 25)		52500
Revaluation reserve (95 − 32.5)		62500
Retained earnings		50200
		360200

Pty		Depn		Reval	
180000		75000	75000		95000
20 000					

OS		SP		Bank	
30000		25000		1 200	
100000				100000	
				25000	

🅮 **16/16 marks awarded** There is a mixture of workings here, but they are done accurately. The 'T' account workings for the rights issue are a little confused and the debits and credits are wrong in places. However, happily for this student, the figures used in the answer are correct so score appropriate marks. Remember that, if a question asks for ledger accounts, then entries must be on the correct sides of the account to score. It is good to see a student using 'T' accounts in the workings. Maximum marks are awarded.

(b) A rights issue is an issue of new shares to the company's shareholders in proportion to the shares that they already own in the company. The shareholders now have more votes at the AGM but if everybody keeps their shares and does not give the right (or sell it) to an outsider the control of the company stays exactly as it was before the rights issue. The shares sold in a rights issue can raise a lot of money, e.g. HBOS in 2008, even though the shares are cheaper than they would have been if they had been bought on the stock market.

A bonus issue is the same as a rights issue except that the shares are given to the shareholders for free. In this case the control of the company definitely does not change because each shareholder gets given more shares in proportion to those they already have. It is sometimes called a capitalisation issue.

It depends on what the directors want whether they make a rights issue or a bonus issue. If the company needs extra finance then they should opt for a rights issue but if they just wish to have less reserves then a bonus issue is better.

ⓔ **5/5 marks awarded** Student A clearly understands the difference between a rights issue and a bonus issue, although the English is not perfect. All the differences are identified and the development of the points is also good.

> **(c)** A rights issue would be made when the company wants to increase its share capital and wishes to raise capital to expand or to buy another company or to buy another piece of expensive machinery. They would make a bonus issue if the reserves were too big for the number of shares already issued in comparison to the asset base of the company.

ⓔ **4/4 marks awarded** This is a good answer and is awarded the full marks.

ⓔ Overall, Student A scores 25 marks, earning a good grade A.

Student B

(a)　　　　　　　**Statement of financial position at 31 Mar 12**

Non-current assets		
Property plant and equipment	200 000	
Depn	75 000	125 000
Current assets		160 200
		285 200
Ordinary shares (30 000 + 125 000 + 77 500)		232 500
Share premium (60 000 – 25 833)		34 167
Revaluation reserve (20 000 – 25 833)		5 833
Retained earnings (50 200 – 25 833)		24 367
		296 867

ⓔ **7/16 marks awarded** This is a good example of a student gaining part marks for showing good, detailed workings. Without the workings in the equity section, no marks would have been earned. But the workings clearly show that Student B has started with the correct figure for ordinary shares and share premium and has correctly calculated the bonus issue on his/her own figures for the issued share capital of 30 000 + 125 000 at 77 500 new shares. Some of the bonus shares have been incorrectly funded by the retained earnings. No workings have been shown for current assets but fortunately for the student the calculation was accurate. Students should always avoid abbreviations: they could cost 'quality of presentation' marks.

> **(b)** A rights issue is given to existing shareholders at a price less than the existing price but a bonus issue is a free issue and the shareholders do not have to pay anything.
>
> 　　They both go to shareholders according to the number of shares they already have so it might be 1 for 3 or 1 for 4.
>
> 　　Bonus shares are better for shareholders because they get more shares free which they can sell and make a profit. If they get an extra share for every three they have they are going to be 1/3 better off than before. It is not so good for the company — they are losing out. They could have sold the shares as a rights issue instead and got more money.

ⓔ **2/5 marks awarded** A couple of good points are made in paragraphs 1 and 2. Student B outlines a common misconception about shareholders being better off. The total worth of their shares stays the same; only the number of shares owned increases — each share being worth proportionately less than before the bonus issue. The English is rather basic.

> **(c)** A rights issue and a bonus issue will be made if the directors cannot afford to pay a dividend.

ⓔ **0/4 marks awarded** This is a poor effort that lacks depth and understanding.

ⓔ Overall, Student B scores 9 marks out of 25 and would not earn a pass at AS.

Question 9 **Ratio analysis**

The following information is available for Tan Lian Sim for the year ended 31 December 2012:

	£
Sales	728 000
Purchases	385 400
Inventory at 1 January 2012	34 600
Inventory at 31 December 2012	35 000
Expenses	265 000
Trade receivables	74 000
Trade payables	30 000
Balance at bank	2 000

All purchases and sales were on credit terms.

Tan Lian is able to provide the following ratios for the year ended 31 December 2011:

Gross profit margin	42.14%
Profit for the year margin	11.03%
Net current asset ratio	2.2:1
Liquid capital ratio	1.7:1
Trade receivables collection period	33 days
Trade payables payment period	32 days
Rate of inventory turnover	11.23 times

(a) **Calculate the same seven ratios for the year ended 31 December 2012 showing clearly the formula used in each case.**   (14 marks)

(b) **Discuss the performance of Tan Lian's business in light of the results for the financial years 2011 and 2012.**   (14 marks)

plus 2 marks for quality of written communication

ⓔ This is a typical 'ratio' type of question. Students must learn the ratios required by the specification and how to calculate the results. Answers must always start with the formula being used. Students must always be aware that comparisons must be made if the results from part (a) are to be useful. In the discussion, the significance of the comparisons must be explained and a conclusion reached as to whether or not there has been an improvement in performance over the two years.

Student A

(a)

Sales		728 000
Inventory	34 600	
Purchases	385 400	
	420 000	
Inventory	35 000	385 000
GP		343 000
Exps		265 000
PfY		78 000

Gross profit margin	$\dfrac{\text{Gross profit}}{\text{Sales}} \times 100$	$\dfrac{343}{728} \times 100 = 47.11\%$	
Profit for the year margin	$\dfrac{\text{Profit for year}}{\text{Sales}} \times 100$	$\dfrac{78}{728} \times 100 = 10.71\%$	
Net current asset ratio	$\dfrac{\text{Current assets}}{\text{Current liabilities}}$	$\dfrac{111}{30}$	$= 3.7:1$
Liquid capital ratio	$\dfrac{\text{Trade receivables} + \text{bank}}{\text{Current liabilities}}$	$\dfrac{76}{30}$	$= 2.53:1$
Trade receivables collection period	$\dfrac{\text{Trade receivables} \times 365}{\text{Credit sales}}$	$\dfrac{74\,000 \times 365}{728\,000}$	$= 38$ days
Trade payables payment period	$\dfrac{\text{Trade payables} \times 365}{\text{Credit purchases}}$	$\dfrac{30\,000 \times 365}{385\,400}$	$= 29$ days
Rate of inventory turnover	$\dfrac{\text{Cost of sales}}{\text{Average inventory held}}$	$\dfrac{385\,000}{34\,800}$	$= 11.06$ times

ⓔ **14/14 marks awarded** This is an excellent response to part (a). Student A prepares the trading section of an income statement at the start of the answer to help give relevant data. Although this probably takes a couple of minutes to prepare, it saves time with the margin calculations and the rate of inventory turnover calculation. No penalties are incurred for using abbreviations in this working.

(b) The gross profit margin has improved in 2012 compared to 2011 — the ratio has increased by almost 12%. This shows that for every £1 of sales Tan made 42 pence in 2011 and 47 pence the following year.

Her profit for the year ratio has deteriorated over the two years but it has only gone down by about 3% from 11.03% to 10.71%. This means that after all expenses have been paid in the first year, out of every £1 sales Tan made just over 11 pence and a year later just under 11 pence.

We can deduce from this that out of every £1 sales the expenses have gone up over the two years. In year 1, 31.11 pence went in expenses, this leapt to 36.4 pence the following year. Are the expenses getting out of control?

The net current asset ratio has almost doubled over the two years. Does this mean that too many resources are being tied up as current assets? If this is so can they be released and changed into non-current assets which might benefit the company more?

The acid test ratio has also gone up significantly — about 50%.

Credit control needs to be tighter. Last year the trade receivable collection and trade payable payment period were about the same. Now Tan is paying her payables in 29 days and waiting to collect money from her receivables for 38 days. Money should always be collected from receivables before payables are paid. It could be due to one huge debtor causing the average receivable collection period to be distorted.

Inventory turnover has stayed much the same but to say whether it is good or bad I would need to know how other businesses are moving their goods.

Conclusion. There are a few worrying signs — gross margin up but profit for year margin down. Liquidity ratios seem to be moving in the wrong direction and Tan needs to improve her credit control.

ⓔ **16/16 marks awarded** This is good analysis based on the limited information available in the question. It is good to see that comparisons are made using terms such as 'improvement' and 'deterioration' and that movements are quantified. The quality of written communication is good and the answer is well structured and easily followed. Maximum marks are scored, earning a grade A.

Student B

(a)

Gross profit margin	$\dfrac{GP}{Sales}$	47.12%
PfY margin	$\dfrac{PfY}{S}$	10.71%
Current ratio CA:CL	3.69:1	
Acid test CA-inv:CL	1.03:1	
Recs collection	$\dfrac{recs \times 365}{Sales}$	38 days
Payables collection	$\dfrac{pays \times 365}{Purchases}$	29 days
Inventory turn	$\dfrac{sales}{inventory}$	20.9 days

ⓔ **4/14 marks awarded** This is a careless response with abbreviations throughout and imprecise formulae. The margins formulae should be multiplied by 100. The incorrect inventory has been used in the current ratio calculation. In the acid test ratio, the inventory has been deducted from receivables plus bank balance.

(b) The gross profit margin is higher in year 2 and is quite good. Expenses have gone up from 31.11% to 36.41% — this is not so good.

The current ratio is far too high it should always be 2:1 and the liquid test is just right it should always be 1:1.

Payable and receivable days should both be 30 days so the receivables are wrong and the payables are just right. Get your receivables to pay up faster give them cash discounts.

> The inventory turn is better: it was being sold every 32.5 days now it is being sold every 20.9 days so that's an improvement of 11.6 days.
> Tan's business is doing OK but some of the ratios are not so good.

ⓔ **5/16 marks awarded** Student B could score more marks by commenting on better or worse performance using own figures from part (a) — 'higher', 'good', 'not so good' are not comparative judgements.

There is no evidence to suggest that expenses have 'gone up'; the proportion of sales being used to pay expenses has gone up.

The student mentions 2:1 and 1:1 as ideal liquidity ratios — this is not so. Ideal ratios vary from sector to sector.

A mark is awarded for quality of written communication and 2 marks are awarded for the comments regarding the rate of inventory turnover based on the student's own calculations and on the increase in relative expenditure on overheads.

ⓔ Overall, Student B earns 9 marks out of 30 — insufficient for a pass grade.

Question 10 **Budgeting and ICT**

The following budgeted figures relate to Plytimb Ltd:

	May	June	July	August	September
	£	£	£	£	£
Sales	30000	40000	42000	44000	50000
Purchases	18000	16000	17000	20000	18000
Wages	14800	15600	15000	15200	16000
Other expenses	4500	4500	5200	4300	4900
Depreciation of non-current assets	3000	3000	3000	3000	3000

Additional information

(1) The cash balance at 1 July is expected to be £200.

(2) 30% of sales will be cash sales.

(3) 50% of credit sale customers will pay in the month following sale, the remainder will pay the following month.

(4) 25% of purchases will be for cash.

(5) Payables will be paid two months after purchase.

(6) Wages will be paid in the month after they are incurred.

(7) Other expenses will be paid for as incurred.

REQUIRED

(a) Prepare a cash budget for each of the three months ending 30 September. (20 marks)

(b) Explain two actions that the managers of a business might take to eliminate a cash deficit shown in one month of a cash budget. (6 marks)

(c) The management of Plytimb Ltd are considering installing ICT in their business. Discuss two benefits that the managers might hope to gain by using ICT to prepare cash budgets. (9 marks)

ⓔ Cash budgets are regularly examined. Separate monthly data must be shown and care must be taken to ensure that items appear in the correct month. Headings must contain the word 'budget' or 'forecast'. The dates covered are in the future so should say a time period 'ending' not ended. The reasons for preparing a cash budget are important as they reveal possible future cash deficits or cash surpluses; students should be aware of actions that managers could take in both circumstances. Students must identify and develop the benefits derived from using ICT for the preparation of cash budgets and should endeavour to stay focused on the question.

Student A

(a) Plytimb Ltd. Cash budget for the three months ending 30 September

	July £	August £	September £
Cash sales	12 600	13 200	15 000
Credit sales	24 500	28 700	30 100
	37 100	41 900	45 100
Less expenses			
Cash purchases	(4 250)	(5 000)	(4 500)
Credit purchases	(13 500)	(12 000)	(12 750)
Wages	(15 600)	(15 000)	(15 200)
Other expense	(5 200)	(4 300)	(4 900)
Cash flow	(1 450)	5 600	7 750
Opening balance	200	(1 250)	4 350
Cash flow	(1 450)	5 600	7 750
Closing balance	(1 250)	4 350	12 100

e **20/20 marks awarded** This is a good answer and scores maximum marks. However, as indicated in the comments to other answers, it is risky not to show any workings. A breakdown of, at least, the income from credit sales into separate receipts for each of the two months should have been shown. If one of the month's receipts had been miscalculated in the above layout, 2 marks per month would have been lost. If they had been shown separately, there is less of a penalty had one month been correct and one incorrect.

There are many different layouts to a cash budget. Student A's version is only one. Stick with the one you feel most comfortable preparing and it will score the marks.

(b) 1 They should try to get their money in from credit sales faster, especially in July.
2 Restructure the payments being made, for example rent or motor expenses, etc. by asking payables to be more patient or just delay the payments for a month or so, but do be careful not to anger the suppliers, they may cut off supplies.

e **4/6 marks awarded** Two acceptable ways of coping with a short-term deficit are listed. Point 1 scores only 1 mark out of 3, as it is lacking development. Student A should have outlined how this policy could be achieved. The second point scores all 3 marks. There is good development, especially about the care to be taken not to alienate suppliers.

(c) 1 Speed. The process will be faster if you use a computer.
2 There are lots of complicated calculations that need to be done, like people not paying for a couple of months.
3 Automatic updating. When the actual figures for cash receipts and payments are known they can be keyed in and the other months will automatically be changed by the computer to take into account the changes in that month and the knock-on effect into later months.
It is a good idea to use ICT because it is faster and more accurate than doing it without a computer.

ℯ 5/9 marks awarded Student A identifies three benefits instead of two. The examiner would read all three and award the marks for the two benefits that score the highest number of marks. Points 1 and 2 identify benefits, but neither is developed sufficiently to score more than a single mark. The third point scores 3 marks.

The student does summarise the discussion but earns only 1 mark — the other 2 marks could have been awarded for development in identifying the specific benefits in preparing a cash budget.

ℯ Overall, Student A scores 29 marks — a marginal grade A. The answer would have benefited from further development in parts (b) and (c).

Student B

(a)

	July £	August £	September £
Balance	200	1750	12650
Incomes			
Cash sales	12600	13200	15000
Credit sales	15000	20000	21000
	20000	21000	22000
Expenses			
Cash purchases	(4250)	(5000)	(4000)
Credit purchases	(18000)	(16000)	(17000)
Wages	(15600)	(15000)	(15200)
Other expenses	(5200)	(4300)	(4900)
Depreciation	(3000)	(3000)	(3000)
Balance c/fwd	1750	12650	26050

ℯ 8/20 marks awarded Student B uses a different, but acceptable, layout from that chosen by Student A. Student B scores 6 marks for cash sales and cash purchases and a single mark for wages and other expenses. A mark is awarded for correct treatment of the opening balance. The closing balance does not score because it is contaminated by the extraneous item 'depreciation' (not a cash expense). The treatment of cash received for credit sales is incorrect. The student has misread the rubric and calculated 50% per month rather than 50% of credit sales, i.e. 35% per month. A similar error is made in calculating credit purchases.

(b) Get your money faster from customers.
Ask the bank for an overdraft.

ℯ 2/6 marks awarded Two valid points are identified, but extra marks could have been scored by developing these points to include strategies to encourage prompt payment and the implications for the business of having an overdraft.

(c) It is more accurate using a computer, they never make mistakes not like people.
Faster. Computers can do things much faster than humans.
So it's a really good idea to use ICT because it never makes mistakes and it speeds things up.

ⓔ **3/9 marks awarded** Two points are identified and a basic summary is given, but all three elements lack development. Remember, points must always be developed if you are to score more than a single mark for any valid point made.

ⓔ Scoring only 13 marks for this answer means that Student B does not achieve a pass mark. More care would ensure more marks and earn this student a comfortable pass grade.

Knowledge check answers

1 False. The term means that there is only one owner. Sole traders can employ as many workers as are necessary to run their business effectively.

2 All partners are responsible for all business debts, no matter how the debt was incurred.

3 The liability of shareholders is limited to the amount they agreed to subscribe for their shares.

4 It should be shown at cost £35 000. Application of the going concern concept.

5 Matching concept.

6 An income statement should show an expense 'Rent £10 000'. In a statement of financial position, under the heading current liabilities, the entry would be 'Other payables £2000'. Application of the accruals (matching) concept.

7 To ensure that information shown in financial statements is reliable, no matter where the statements are produced or who produces them.

8 The private running costs should be treated as drawings.

9 'Trade receivables' is the term used for a group of individual trade debtors.

10 The balance shown in the provision for doubtful debts account should be £420. So £20 should be entered as an expense in the income statement for the year.

11 Both accounts should appear in a general ledger. Application of the prudence concept.

12 False. Both methods apportion the cost of a non-current asset over its useful lifetime, but use a different method of calculating the annual cost.

13 False. The carrying amount shows the cost of a non-current asset less aggregate depreciation charged to date.

14 At the end of year 2 the charge using the straight-line method would be £10 000; the charge using the reducing balance method would be £8000. Reported profits would be £2000 greater using the reducing balance method.

15 Profit of £4000.

16 Both purchases of office equipment are examples of capital expenditure. Payment of an insurance premium is revenue expenditure. The purchase of a private car is not a business expense and, if business finance was used, it would be included as drawings.

17 A rights issue is used by a company to raise additional capital from existing shareholders. A bonus issue is funded by capitalising reserves.

18 Net current asset ratio 4.1:1. Liquid current ratio 1.4:1.

19 Average collection period (or trade receivables collection period) is 28 days (27.375 days).

20 Gearing ratio = £100 000 + £50 000/£350 000 + £100 000 + £50 000 + £70 000 + £280 000 = £150 000/£850 000 = 17.6% Low geared since the ratio is less than 50%

21 Limitations include: use of past, historic, data; a total detailed picture of business activities is not evident from financial information only; different business types, sizes, structures, accounting policies etc; problems of making 'like with like' comparisons.

22 We cannot say. There are no data from which we may draw comparisons.

23 The benefits would include: planning future development of the business; co-ordinating the objectives of individual departments; encouraging a dialogue between departments; making beneficial decisions for the business as a whole; using budgets as a control mechanism.

24 Budgetary control delegates financial planning to managers. It is an evaluative tool. Performance of managers is continually judged by comparing actual results with those set in their departmental budget.

25 Limitations would include: preparation from inaccurate or easily achievable data; if imposed from 'above' budgets can act as demotivators; can lead to unhealthy competition and rivalries.

Note: **bold** page numbers indicate definitions of key terms.

AQA AS Accounting